DOWNLOADS
from
Heaven

by
ALISON RYAN-CHASE

To Auntie Mary

May these poems bless
and encourage you

love Alison

AR.

Conscious Dreams
PUBLISHING

Downloads From Heaven

Copyright © 2024: Alison Ryan-Chase

First Printed in United Kingdom 2024

Published by Conscious Dreams Publishing
www.consciousdreamspublishing.com

Edited by Elise Abram
Cover Designed by Emily's World of Design
Typeset and ebook formatting by Amit Dey

ISBN: 978-1-915522-93-1 (paperback)

In Loving Memory of Dawne

Dawne made me recognise my gift and inspired me
to become an author.
Her love for life and her passion to encourage and
empower will always be remembered.

Table of Contents

Last Dance

The death of a loved one is like listening to the melody
and lyrics of your favourite song coming to its end
The feeling is hard to comprehend.
The reality hits with the last note...
She's gone
No longer does she dance
Sing to the music of life
No longer a twinkling of light
But has entered through the gate
Welcomed by many gathered at His throne
I take comfort in knowing she's not alone

I remember days when we were young
Summer holidays filled with fun
She taught me Double-Dutch
Man, she skipped with class
Constant jokes rolled out her mouth
When I got in serious trouble
Laughing, she said, "Giiirrrrl, your ass is grass"
She also spoke words of wisdom
It was inevitable she would reach God's Kingdom

Always sat me down and began her lecture to encourage
and motivate
Open my eyes to let me see

Then she wrote a book called *Giving Birth to Me*
What an awesome testimony and a guide to live your best life,
How to escape a negative mindset, put yourself in position to survive
Dawne really showed the benefits to living positive and thrive.

She shared how we had gifts within us like a pregnancy
That we needed to nurture our bodies and clear our minds
and then we'd find what lies in our innermost.
And when the time comes, waters break and Push
With everything, Push

And watch your ideas be born.

You accomplished writing your books
In the background I stood and looked.
Seeing the creativity in me, you encouraged me to write my own
So from you the seed was sown
Now here I am
Finally an author
I give credit and dedicate this first book to you
Although saddened you are not here
I know your spirit sings with joy in the heavenly atmosphere

Thank you, Dawne, for constantly pushing me
To open doors leading to my promised destiny

Rest In Peace, Cousin.

Introduction

It is true what the word of God says to 'Keep your heart with all diligence, for out of it springs the issues of life' (Proverbs 4:23).

I have truly been careful with my heart. Though my life has faced many highs and just as many lows, it has been broken and healed.

Over the years, I have been in a position of prayer... 'My soul longs, yes, even faints for the courts of the Lord, my heart and my flesh cry out for the living God' (Psalms 84:2), and faithfully, He answered me, downloading words that beautified the pages I placed them on.

Sometimes, the cry is not outward, but a softening in the spirit in the stillness of peace where my thoughts run away with me, and what is inside flows out like a trickling stream that reaches the mouth of the river.

As the world's turmoil grows, it is in earnest that we tell lost souls about the soon coming King, to turn from their ways and be adopted by Our Father in Heaven, born again in a new creation in Christ. 'Jesus answered and said to him, "Most assuredly, I say to you, unless one is born again, he cannot see the Kingdom of God"' (John 3:3).

There are two parallels in our being: we live, and we die. The loss of my dearly beloved brother was and still is the hardest thing I have ever faced. With rhythmical words, I have cried out on paper the utter brokenness, the despair, and the missed birthdays and years. Never did I know grief could be so suffocating, but God is the air I breathe, and His strength keeps me standing.

I pray that as I share the impact of his death, the love of siblings shall move you to love and appreciate your family.

My health has taken a knock back a few times, and I have been admitted into hospital on quite a few occasions. Although I was ill, the people around me were fellow patients suffering from their own ailments; I always found a way to capture the presence of God and relax by putting pen to paper and sharing the environment of the ward. These times were sad, but during sadness, there was always room for a smile.

As you guide through this collection of poetry, my prayer is that it will warm your heart and stir your soul to realise it's only in Jesus Christ that you are made whole. Dance with the melody of my words, look at the world and smile.

*And He said to her, 'Daughter, your faith has
made you well. Go in peace and be healed
of your affliction.'*

Mark 5:34

1
HOSPITAL
AND RECOVERY

Imitation of life

Listening to a rhythm of breathing apparatus... like an engine room of a ship, six beds either side each hoping the other doesn't capsize
Earlier, family members gathered around, standing there with agonising frowns, all having something to say,
The rhythm of the engine pulling them in an uneasy sway.
They look at each other wondering
'Is today the day?'

Violins and cellos begin to play in their hearts,
standing, their silhouettes dressed in a shade of blackness,
in a state of unawareness....no realisation their loved one isn't even dead yet!!
The engine still running, opening their lungs to get life in.
The rhythm is in time and the drum of the heart is still beating.

Bed 1... moved twice for the day, no relatives came her way. Got up sprightly at every mealtime and slept in between... breathing nicely.

Bed 2... walks ten steps to the loo and comes back fighting for air, grabs a mask in desperation. Lungs gurgling music in a mess, no timing, no rhyming, no melody, pure distress...

Husband looks in her eyes and talks her through what to do. Together he paces her step by step ...in...out...in...out...' that's it, darling'
In through your nose and out through your mouth. Breathing apparatus continues the job alone.

Bed 3... Sweet Alice, older than all of us added together in the room. Spoon fed, doesn't move, I suspect will see the King's palace soon.

Bed 4... What a racket! What a snore! But, poor darling, it's not natural breathing, it's the suction to pull the air through the plastic, for her little frame is quite drastic. What a struggle! What a roar...! The noise itself becomes therapeutic and relaxes oneself.

Bed 5... praise God, survived, jumped ship and walked out the door.

Bed 6... well, no breathing apparatus for me; I get shortness of breath, panic, then use the noisy rhythm of the room to set me straight.
I look around this room with four other souls fighting for a life extension,
cannot sleep for their music is not my type and the beat can often put you in fright... so...
I write...
I pray...
I read my words...

Thank you is the thought that comes to mind
Thank You, Jesus, for the natural air You gave me to breathe, after a trim 44 years, still allowing a heartbeat. Natural rhythm even in a fight for my airway, God still has control.
I am His and His alone.

Bed 4... just had a shutdown. Panic is all around. Apparatus starts to quit, Valarie starts to fit... 'NURSE, NURSE,' I start to shout, jump out me bed, run fast, get help, run back and rub her legs, 'Calm yuhself, sweetie, help is on the way.'

Nurses run fast, I step out the way... what else do I do???? Stretch my hands and start to pray...

'Not today.'

And not today, it surely is, for the Spirit of the Lord passed with a kiss.
Gone is the humdrum of all the apparatus. Val just needed reassurance and to open her mouth, breathe in... out... in... out...
No imitation of life, just the giver of life giving yet another chance.
In the morning, I pray she'll get up and dance.

The Visit

She sleeps...
So soundly
All day
Propped up on a starched white pillow
Her silver-grey hair frames a childlike face
She smiles in her sleep with angelic grace
Silently sleeps
No tosses, no turns
She doesn't cry out
Not even yawns
Is she alive? I wonder as she doesn't even moan
You'd think being in hospital she might groan
Her colour a mixture... well don't laugh...
But truly shades of grey!
Edna... Edna the nurse calls,
Edna, your lunch, my darling
Sit up and try to eat
There is a slight movement within her sheets
She shuffles up using her hands and feet
With every effort her frail arm reaches across
Takes two spoonfuls and a sip of tea
Quietly she slips back into the comfort of her pillow
No more of that food she wishes to swallow
She sleeps
So soundly

The noises of other patients
The busyness of the ward
Does nothing to disturb this lil angel of the Lord
A few hours later, Edna opens her eyes
Oh the sparkle at the sight of her surprise
She literally squeals in delight
The woman who slept as still as a corpse
Now sits up effortlessly
All ready to talk
Her colour... Yes, a mixture, but shades of the rainbow
What, you wonder, has changed her so
To such a high from being so low?
I tell you it was something so simple
And not an expensive spend
It was a visit from a very dear old friend
They chatted, they giggled, they reminisced
No longer frail, still, alone and forgotten
But filled in spirit, loved and remembered
They chatted for well over an hour
Her friend bid farewell and her cheek she kissed
Edna waved bye-bye and gently closed her eyes
She fell asleep mumbling as if still awake
As she drifted off, her fingers fluttered
Her mind still in conversation with words she had not time
to share
Her friend has now left her in the doctors' and nurses' care
There... there... she sleeps soundly
But somehow the ambience around her is less lonely
Her sleep looks like peace and not of near death

Good heavens she makes a noise...She actually snores
One visit but it brings fresh stillness
Fresh angelic grace
A peace above understanding
An innocence of a child
Sleep now, Edna
You will be well in a little while.

"Come What May"...

As they say
My smile they cannot take away
From the rising of the sun
To the going down of the same
I forever will end a prayer in Yeshua's name
Tired of paying doctors' bills
Block your ears from the voice saying you are ill
Hush be still

For I know poor health is not our Father's will
He came to give life and in abundance fill
So how did you start your day?
Did you give Him thanks for waking you up...
You know... Pray?!
Did you stop for a moment to meditate?
To listen, to hear what He had to say?

Do you believe...?
He alone can change a diagnosis
And give to you a prognosis so accurate
It leaves those with a doctorate
Baffled and no choice but to declare,
They have witnessed a Spiritual move in the atmosphere
Professionals said, 'No way'

God said, 'My way'
And the patient lifted up their hands and cried
'Yahweh'

Believe in God for your healing...
Come what may.

Be encouraged

And said, 'If you diligently heed the voice of the Lord your God and do what is right in His sight, give ear to His commandments and keep all His statutes, I will put none of the diseases on you which I have brought on the Egyptians. For I am the Lord who heals you.'

Exodus 15:26

He is Mighty to Save...

Katherine calls out 'Jane Jane!'… So much anguish so much pain—what is the story behind that name, Jane?

Elizabeth quarrels time and time again…
'Where's my tablets? It's a blinking shame.
It's been four hours that I've been asking—you lot should be ashamed.'
'We come in 'ere to get better but deteriorate each day.
Is that what the NHS has come to?
Gor blimey, not in my day!'

Linda is wet again, and her quarrelling drives the nurses insane...
'Oy what time's dinner?
Oy what time's tea?
Oy when the blinkin' 'eck are yuh gonna change me???'

The nurse tries the nurse sighs—
She's in it up to her eyes
Demands coming from every bed and she shakes her head
Every one of the staff team claiming they have something else to do
For Pete's sake, how many of allyuh want to go on a tea break?

Every job is 'no-one's' job, but nobody knows who 'no-one' is!!!
So jobs go undone...what trouble is dis??!!

Dearest Brenda bows her head uncomfortably on her chest,
Struggles to swallow her food and all she wants to do is rest.
Physio comes and bugs her, 'Brenda. Pleeeeease swallow, or surely a six-foot hole will follow

Sweet Tess always seems to be sitting in her mess, waiting...
'Nurse Nurse, need the bed pan...
Nurse Nurse, okay maybe the commode...
Nurse Nurse, give me something to take me further away from the hearse!
Again, for assistance she rings the call bell with persistence—
I know the nurse station are aware, for I hear it bleeping in the distance.

Awwww there are also nice things to see
Like beautiful Margaret across from me.
A lovely lass that was on a trip from Scotland and rudely interrupted by a fall—
Ended up in Wexham...
Please pray for her to be healed quickly and be on her way
So she can enjoy the rest of her holiday.

Oh Jean... always cold, in her bed like a foetus she folds.
Constantly whimpers...'Why am I here, why was I born,
what's the purpose of my life??? Ever since childhood I've
been riddled with strife.'
I go over and gently rub her back and speak in her ear how
much Jesus loves thee
And not everything in life is made clear for us to see.

'Remember *The Sound of Music*, Jean, when she sang about
feeling sad?
Just put your mind on happy things, Jean, not the terrible
and the bad.'

Today is Sunday and the earth is still filled with His Glory
Songs fill my heart as the Holy Spirit truly breaks out.

Beth & Katherine are still, not a word do they shout
Linda is dry, resting and eased off the pestering
Margaret sits in her chair and still filled with good cheer...
Could be the quiet noise of praise & worship songs I have
playing in the air

Brenda lifted her hands (yayyy) and poured a cup of
water—
I pray before she leaves this life
She gets a hold of the 'Living Water!'
Tess is lying quietly beside me and every so often leans
over and chats to me.
She's dry

She's tidy
She's a lovely lady
Saviour
He can move mountains
Our God is Mighty to save.
Forever Author of Salvation
Jesus arose and conquered the grave
Amen
#justanotherdayatwexhamhosp

Patient Patient

It's a scenery not often sought
Gifts of juice, fruit and cakes friends have brought
The sounds of nurses' bells ringing
Monitors in synchronized chiming
Drs offloading information to patients and families earnestly
awaiting…

Can I please go home?
It's time I leave
Pack me some medication,
That I don't mind to receive

Agnes, dearest, it's not yet time
Let's place your bed by the window,
Feel the sunshine
The clouds slowly glide across the sky
Shades of grey mixed with shades of white
All, however, lined with a glorious light
The warmth of the sun brings her comfort as it touches
her face
Trees dancing in the distance
Swaying in unison and grace
No, this is not the ideal place
But God turns it around so His love you can taste

In all the confusion of mind
There is one thing in hospital you can find
People who need a friend for a moment
Just to get them through their escaped tears
Tears of loneliness, feelings of despair
Released by kind words from a stranger
Letting you know they may not know you, but they care
Speaking kind words stripping away critical symptoms and
threat of danger
Instilling words of affirmation for good health, swift
recovery,
A healing miracle for all around to see
No matter where you are in life
God can always see...
Near you He'll always be
Waiting for you to reach out and touch His garment
Years of illness shall halt
Face ceased being seasoned with salt

Today, looking out the window nine floors up
Is the day your tears filled His cup
Which in turn poured out onto you just as you were about
to give up
"No my child
As old as you are
You will still be My daughter
There's no need for despair
Rest your head on your pillow
A good report from your doctor will follow

And soon...
Very soon
You'll be discharged out of there."

The view from your window
Brings to you a smile
And the calmness that follows
Helps you to lean back and gently sigh...
Today is not the day to meet the sweet by-and-by

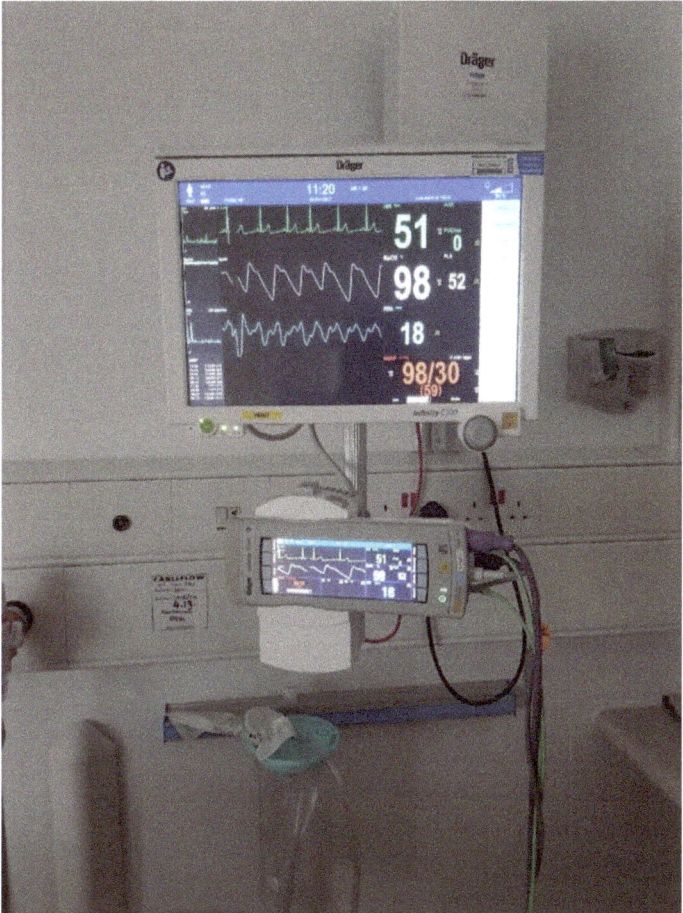

The Sun Still Shines

It's a beautiful day
Clouds are puffy
But the sun still shines
Someone got bad news
Their loved one died
Their world just broke...
But the sun still shines

Someone got good news
They've passed a test
And jump in jubilee
For their future now seems bright
Yes, on this same day
There is also delight
And the sun still shines.

Up on the ward
Four beauties keep company
Sunita is stuck immobilised in her bed
She has hope when she sees me walk

Positive words to her I daily talk
So she smiles when I look her way

It's still a beautiful day
And the sun still shines

Sylvie Sylvie
All she wants to do is drink tea
Disagrees with every nurse
If her tongue could move more
I'm sure she'd curse
Bless her Lord
Catch her tears from thoughts of past years
Show her daily Your love in signs
Let her know the sun still shines

Jeanne sleeps so still
Like a mannequin
Rather than a tired old lady so ill
When she sleeps, show her, Lord
All the things You have in store
Let her dreams be of mansions
And golden doors
One with her name engraved,
For in her sleep, she cried out to be saved
Even in her darkest of days
The sun still shines

Elenore, my little lady next door
Never sleeps and stares at the floor

Eat, Elenore, eat, but she shouts back
NO MORE
I DON'T WANT POTATOES
I DON'T WANT PORRIDGE
I DON'T WANT ENSURE
LEAVE ME ALONE
I DON'T WANT TO MOVE MY JAW
She doesn't care, her body is sore
Blood pressure sky-high
It knocks on Death's door
Drink Elenore drink, your mouth is so dry
The doctors and nurses stand and sigh

How, Lord, do you encourage someone to live when
they've given up?

Tell me what to say, God
Fill her empty cup
Straighten out her frown
Open her eyes that are wide shut
As I sit beside the window
The light makes me a silhouette
Let it be she sees the Holy host
Her first encounter that stirs her innermost
May the beauty of outside help her see
There is much more to live for
Her time is not yet
Restore her appetite, let her not fret
For today someone grieved

Someone laughed
Someone received
Someone danced
Someone sang
Someone's life has begun

As I sit patiently in this ward
Praising God as my health is restored
I glance out the window

And the first thing that came to my mind,
NO matter what the day held for you...
The sun still shines

Stroke v Migraine

I'm so mad
Feel so sad
I want to cry
But my eyes are dry
You see, I've watched on telly
About a young woman's plight
Her journey to health
Not one of wealth
But it's the care and attention
I am grieved to mention

She had a stroke at age thirty-four
Doctors and neurologists worked hard for a cure
I think of myself, there was no open door,
Hemiplegic migraines, no-one heard of before

She says she was lost inside herself
Lost in her body
Yet I was lost in an open room
Left on a shelf, it was like an open tomb.
She speaks of her stroke and the effects it's had
I think that was the thing that made me sad...
Knowing as she described all the symptoms,
I thought, 'Oh my gosh, someone has what I have.'

But no, she didn't
She got neurological help
Occupational therapy,
Physiotherapy,
Speech therapy,
Experimental tests...
She went through the lot trying to obtain normal function
of her brain
Functions she had lost like me
Yet I received an alarm pendant
She lost like me, but we were not the same
She had a stroke
I had a migraine

It made her more important
I was just sunshine trying to push through the rain
They say I had no brain damage
And I'd be restored in time
But there was damage within me
My life's ambition slipping away
Word-finding hard
Concentration levels slow
No indication of which way my life's going to go

She gave a speech to therapists in a room
Who clapped as she finished and smiled at the applause...
Funny, I did the same thing too in Queen Square
Neurological Hospital,
To a room filled with therapists

Who looked at me like I was taking the pi**
They asked questions that made me uneasy
Insinuating they thought I was crazy.
I didn't see them react like that to the other lady
She had lost the same functions as me
But not the same
She'd had a stroke
They struggled when mines were called a migraine.

'You'll get over it
Go home and rest
Don't work
Don't study
Don't clean any mess
Don't think
Don't talk
Don't stress'
Have I become the neurologist's pest?
Do they look at me and laugh in jest?

I didn't see them do that to her...
That woman who'd spoken about those symptoms that
changed her life
Symptoms like me but regarded not the same
For she had a stroke
Me - I had a hemiplegic migraine
The divide in the name
Neurologist declared 'similar'

But measured by straws
I drew the one shorter

And like sunshine trying to pierce through the rain
I sit in the midst of pain
Remembering my Healer is the Great Author
Jesus is His name
So yes, we are similar, but I am definitely not the same
For I am saved by His grace
Redeemed of past disgrace
I look up to see His face

She has the Neurologist and top-notch medical care
I have God's Son and the victory has been won
From these symptoms I have recovered
He said I am His beloved
This experience is rare
And it broke my heart to see
How the world is so unfair
But I chose to share with you and let you know
That if you openly bare to Him what grieves you within
He will show how much He cares
And make your life worth living

So to all those who passed me by
Classed me as unimportant because...
I was diagnosed with a common name
I am eternally grateful that stroke was not my pain

Yes, migraine was the trigger
This good news I must deliver
Even though a bag was given with thirty pieces of silver
The Messiah is still the winner
He died, rose again and lives for me and every other sinner

I will never be the same
In Jesus Christ Almighty's name

2

BE ENCOURAGED, BE FREE

⸎⸎

Salvation belongs to the Lord.
Your blessing is upon Your people

Psalms 3:8

⸎⸎

Psalm 3:8

When last have you read the psalmist's words?
What did you receive from it? What have you heard?

A sweet voice charmed his brain
His hand could not hold back restrain
So, he put ink to paper again and again,
That we in the future will not be ashamed,
Be broken-hearted or live by ill-gotten gain.
That we may look to the Psalms for comfort and joy,
And foil the devil with his plan to destroy.
satan will try to use us like puppets,
But remember we are not his toys.

King David fell, stood up, fell and shook up.
An adulterer, a liar, a betrayer and a murderer.
Yes, he sinned greatly but not repeatedly.
His heart and unchangeable faith were with God
And he was delivered.

A killer of giants, an ancestor of our Lord and Saviour
Jesus Christ.
A shepherd himself and a great poet
Because of his obedience to God's voice telling him to write,

We can live today, we can learn, we can pray, we can praise
We can laugh, we can dance as David danced,
God does give us a chance.

He hears our prayers, knows our fears.
What can God possibly hold back from you?
A heart and soul that repents and bares all...
Is someone/something after you like David had Saul?
Bill collectors, unpaid fines, abusive husbands, cantankerous wives,
Huge mortgage payments, drugs, alcohol or fine wines??

God can and WILL deliver you from all.

Psalms is you
Psalms is me
It's part of who we are and where we are destined to be.
Our deepest thoughts and prayers
Our deepest pain, our deepest shame

But as we stand and declare our love for our Heavenly King
As we let out what we so tightly hold in
God will open our eyes and remind us we are HIS kin
We are children of God
Brothers and sisters in Christ.

Rejoice, laugh, shout, let it all out
We're not puppets but pliable clay
Let the Potter have His way.

From the Lord comes deliverance. May your blessing be on
your people.

Amen

My One Desire

Aspire to aim higher is my one desire
The Vision of my destination
Awakens a warm sensation
But the journey is not always easy
Distractions hurdle like balls of fire.

I'm stretching out, my arm's losing power
My heart cries and my energy dies
It's in my reach
Holding onto the positive words my pastor preached... I rise

There is something powerful God wants to place in my hand
Something no one else can lift as they stand
His will in me I must fulfil
No devil in hell has the ability to keep me still

Before me looks desolate
Trials and burdens in the way of my path
Conflict with mind and Spirit
A battle with body and soul
Can I do it?

Can this diamond shine from soft, fragile coal?
Yes... beauty comes forth from this black gold

A testimony shall arise
Out of Darkness is the glory of a sunrise.
The colours dance in the sky as morning breaks

The birds in the trees sing with the angelic orchestra that
plays in the wind
The branches dance
My eyes look up and glance
I glance a vision of hope
My God has distilled in me the antidote
And it covers me in a multitude of colours like Joseph's
multicoloured dream coat

I shall stand and take that step
The other foot shall surely follow
Before you know it, I will be walking into my destiny
Breathe in, exhale and pace the journey
A change in position will increase velocity

Then all will see what God placed inside of me
I shall wait, I shall not be afraid
The word of God quietens my spirit as I rest...

For the vision is yet for an appointed time;
But at the end it will speak, and it will not lie.
Though it tarries, wait for it;
Because it will surely come, It will not tarry.

Habakkuk 2:3

Life is a journey... I'm still on it

It's Not Yours to Hold

ELIF:
Your mind boggles! But you just can't let go, the world has you bowing at its feet,
Doing the wrong things seem too sweet, habits dangle in front of you like they are a treat
You are so weak when you stand to your feet.
You are all alone, just can't realise your soul's in defeat.

FELI:
Still unsure?... Can you really not see through all your tears?
You blame God for your trials and fears.
Don't you realise He sent His Son to set the captives free?
It doesn't matter to Him where you've been or what you've done,
His Son rose from the dead to help you overcome,
Not to see you live your life constantly on the run...
And anyway, who or what are you running from?
Or more to the point, do you know to whom you are running?

IFEL:
Think it's a foreign language?
Don't get it yet?

At some point in time,
An athlete not properly trained,
Can run out of breath and be left behind by the rest.
The muscles cramp and the runner collapses crippled to the ground.
No matter how much they try to rise, they fail, they cannot connect,
There is a defect!

LIFE:
Aha!! You got it...
Or are you still adrift?
How well are you running your race?
Are you spinning around on a merry-go-round, humming a merry tune?
Skipping around in a childish game,
Not aware that you are singing the words, 'You've been framed.'

Or are you chillin' and walking slow?
A 'know it all' and you've set your own flow...
Geniuses at the obstacle race—no way will you fall flat on your face!!

LIFE... It's not yours to hold
LIFE... It's not yours to control
LIFE... How long do you think you got?
What are you going to do?
What are you going to say?

On that day, when it's your turn for God to put you on the 'hot spot'?
Who do you entrust your life to?
Who do you thank with praise & worship when the right things come your way?
Is it your Heavenly Father, the Holy Trinity??
Did you thank Him for the life of His Son?
Who bled for the living dead, for converted unbelievers who saw the blind man see?
He hung high on the cross of Calvary to save every sinner like you and me.

... Or was you too hungover from the night before?
You know... remember? When you stumbled through the bedroom door—
Did you even make it that far, or did you wake lying in vomit next to your car?

So, you've given your life to the darkness of this world, unknowingly
Not realizing that blindness leads to a wrong kind of eternity,
Having the wrong sense of confidence that you could live your life fast until the day came...
And just before your last breath ...
Switch over the controller with opened eyes. Oh what a shame!

Well, this is the thing,
Your life's bell will eventually ring!!
No-one knows the day or the hour,
and certainly not YOU, my friend.

Open your eyes NOW, don't wait till the end,
Open your heart, let me sow the seed.

LIFE...
When there is nothing left but God, that is when you will realise—
GOD is all you need.

My First Testimony as a Born-Again Christian

In Jan 1999, I suffered a stroke... I was 29 years old. I totally lost my speech, motor and thinking skills. I had limited movement in my right limbs, short-term memory loss, tinnitus in both my ears. I had vertigo and I couldn't drive anymore. I became a new single mum to three children. I also forgot how to cook completely. I had been a chef for the past twelve years. It was a very scary time of my life and I was registered as disabled.

I felt lost and thought my life would never be the same. The neurologists at Queen Square Hospital said although they were scholars of the brain, the brain is such a complex organ that not even they know all there is to know and gave no guarantees that I'd recover.
No... that wasn't encouraging!

Five months later, I received salvation and became a born-again Christian in the Pentecostal faith and started to attend the Potter's House Christian Fellowship; it was the beginning of my healing.

Initially, it took two and a half years with speech therapy, prayer and faith for my speech and other symptoms to be restored. But it all began the day I gave my life to Jesus. Oh, there have been MANY trials along the way (never believe anyone who says life is a bed of roses after a prayer of salvation) and I suffered a few more TIA episodes, although not as bad as the first.

Eventually, in 2009, I was diagnosed with a condition called hemiplegic migraine [1]The symptoms are brought on by extreme stress! I was in a turbulent marriage at the time and worked three jobs, seven days a week, so… Umm… figures!!!

There were certain people who came into my life at the time that tried to keep me sick, but God took control. Then I gained control of my mind by sifting out negativity and positively gave and focused on others weaker in the faith. I've had to learn to take control of my mind, and with God's help, it has been possible.
I am a survivor.

My testimony is sooooo long. I need more than a couple of pages!
It is not the first time I've shared my testimony, but someone reading this needs to be encouraged.

You CAN control your thoughts, allow God to conform your mind to His. Think, 'What would Jesus do? ' And

---

[1] transient ischaemic attack (mini stroke)

let go of the negativity that could eventually kill you emotionally, spiritually and physically.

Your creator created your mind; He will help you master it.

Change the Way You Think

I had no idea I could control my thoughts or choose which thoughts I focused on and believed in.

I had the power to stop mental, emotional, financial, physical and sexual abuse. You can choose to think and focus on healing thoughts, beautiful, positive thoughts, 'And do not be conformed to this world, but be transformed by the renewing of your mind, that you may prove what is that good and acceptable and perfect will of God' (Romans 12:2 NKJV).

Change the way you think.

Say, God, I want to experience Your power in my mind; I choose to focus on Your goodness, mercy, grace and Your love for me. No matter what negative thought comes my way, I know that You are so much bigger and better, and I cast it out in the matchless name of Jesus Christ. Be my guide and help me to always find joy.

What makes me happy today? The thought that this marks twenty-two months not being in hospital once with a hemiplegic attack. Seventeen months in a row with perfect speech.

Hallelujah!

Oh My Gosh! How could I forget to add that I taught myself how to cook again and am now the proud personal chef of a fine dining business I'm working on. It's on Instagram as @palys_g2_9. Take a look in your spare time if you'd like.

Be encouraged.

Dear Lord,

I give You my hands to do Your work,
my feet to go Your way,
my eyes to see as You see,
my tongue to speak Your words,
my mind that You may think in me,
my spirit that You may pray through me.
I give you all of me, that your light can shine through me.
Above all,
I give You my heart so that You may love through me.
Lord, I give myself to You,
so that You can use me.

Amen

The Journey Home

The atmosphere is thick
All around are heartbeats
Lungs faithfully competing
Keeping up the rhythm to breathe in and exhale

We stand

For all the seats are taken with tired souls
Their day was long and there was much to behold
There's a noise of chattering voices
Wanting desperately to share
Their experience of their day and revealing their
choices...

Their choices
Their walk
Their personal walk
They talk and talk and talk
Some with laughter
Some with sorrow
For they know not what will happen tomorrow

I stand

I hold on to the bar and close my eyes
There's a noise
It's the clanging of the engine
The rolling of the train
It's the echo of the tunnel
It's the sound of thunderous rain

I also hear a chorus
That encamps all around us
A sound of a heavenly realm
A swarm of angels in exaggerated praise
With open mouths and trumpets blown
The sound increases as my spirit releases
And more and more I hear a glorious outpouring of noise

I hear voices but I cannot speak
With my eyes wide shut I see my arms raised
In my imagination I lift my voice and exalt the One who came
To die for me to set me free
Daily, yes, He walks with me
Showing me all He has for me

His will

His purpose
His praise
And then I realise...

The noise I hear is captive within me
My body, soul and spirit singing and rejoicing in harmony
Just the knowledge that I know
God is forever with Me.

Great is the Lord, and greatly to be praised;
And His greatness is unsearchable

−Psalms 145:3

And what is the exceeding greatness of His power
toward us who believe, according to the working
of His mighty power

−Ephesians 1:19

Slowly Wins the Race

Slowly
But surely from the depth of the deep
We rise and to God we seek
His goodness, grace and mercy
Everlasting to Everlasting
He reminds us continuously
We are His children, and we are royalty
Even in sickness and pain
He is there in the midst of it all
Answering the call of healing
Whether it's immediate or in limitations
Speak highly to Him in meditation

His word is true from Genesis to Revelation
Yes, the Bible is our balm and medication
So, when your body doesn't work how it was made
And the devil taunts you to grow afraid
Lay down at the altar, call on His name
Let your spirit intercede on your behalf
Stand in your armour
Head high without shame
Shake off the lies

Jump up
Wave your hands and praise
Healing comes in Jesus' name
Believe you are delivered
Even if every day you feel the same
He knits you back carefully and precisely
From the depths of the deep
Goodness, grace and mercy is ours to keep
Be aware of your tongue, positively speak
And before you know it
You've been made whole
No cracks
Yes, glory to God, you have won the attack
Now renewed and filled with the Spirit
Your testimony will touch others
It's worth being told.

Be encouraged

Wrong Turns

When the road is long
And you travel whistling a song,
Where there are bends and turns
Bumps on unlevel ground
The shadows of the mountains echo a sound.

Looking at the snow-ridged peaks
Like Moses, you climb to seek.
Leaving the road, you let down your load
Taking yourself in another direction,
Prayers insisting on Our Father's protection.
But the paths split in different sections...
Which way will you go?

You cry, 'Lead me, Father, lead me home.
Carry me over that I may see and seal my belief,
That You are truly my company walking through this
mountain range.'

Slipping on the rocks; stumbling on the loose pebbles.

It's then you realise that you've turned from the road God
had for you, leading to your destiny.

You bow down desperately, crying out once again, Lord,
rescue me.

Then the breeze sings back a song
That even though you have done wrong
The Father's love will never change
He'll lead you back upon the road
Straight ahead with a few bends and turns.
Declaring no more shall curiosity lead you astray

Your debt, He whispers, He's already paid.
So nothing should really get in your way.
But if you come upon another mountain range,
Keep your head straight.
Let God lead you,
Slowing down only to be still, listening to know His will.

The devil played upon Jesus on the highest rocks

Tempting Him to give up His inheritance,
So like the Father's Son, your heart shall revere God's
name on every occasion
Just believe and in every situation,
Speak out the scriptures, for there is power in declarations.

Overcome by casting out doubt and hesitation
Covering yourself in the Bible from Genesis to Revelation.

Interlude

Sometimes, I look at life and really appreciate the seasons of each year that passes by. We, too, operate like nature and go through our four seasons that coincide with spring, summer, autumn and winter. It can be a rollercoaster, resembling being bipolar! When we are up, we are at the top of our game, everything going swell, but when things are low, it goes rock bottom before we can bounce back up.

I've learnt to take time out in each atmosphere I find myself. God finds me in a quiet place and the words from heaven download deep inside my soul, and all I can do is start writing, start typing, dressing each word to form a musical sentence, and before you know it, a poem is formed.

I read back what I've produced, and I can only come to one conclusion… the words, idea, the topic must have come from the Holy Spirit. So, I give all the glory to God for the marvellous things He has done for using me as a vessel to touch lives. To turn people's hearts towards God. To be inquisitive about salvation.

Sometimes, I play. Test God in a way, I tell myself, 'Think of a word,' and then proceed to write a poem based upon and using that word. One hundred per cent of the time it works, and it is so much fun reading it back and being in awe how God does that.

Downloads from heaven, essence from my heart, stirred together to produce God's work of art.

As you continue to read, I pray I plant a seed, that roots may grow and in due time you will come to know the Father, Son and Holy Ghost.

The beauty of buds in spring

The summer sun this season brings

Breeze that whistles through autumn leaves

The coldness and expectation of snow slips in winter with ease

I sit, I smile and for a little while, it's just me and Jesus

Nothing comes between us.

He looks into me and then He'll whisper and say,

'Write, my child, for by you I shall have My way

And let somebody reading

Meet with Me today.'

3
TRANSFORMATION

Woman of God

No other can pour out love like a shower
No other perfume so fragrant,
No other rose
No other flower
No other I know with such Holy Ghost power

She stands with elegance
She stands with purpose
She stands with vision, never loses focus
She stands for God, forever praising her Lord
She stands in armour and hand on her sword

Woman of God, they call her, all that know her

Her beauty glows inside out
Filling hearts as she declares God's love
And she is loved more than she knows
From the crown of her head
To the tips of her toes
Sharing the gospel with strangers and those she knows
Leaving her sweet fragrance called Christ wherever she goes

Is she you?
Are you marvelled by God who first formed you?

Moulded you in your mother's womb
As you grew and gave your life to Christ,
Learning to speak to others all things nice.
Words of conviction and helping grieving hearts
Helping others to erase negativity and putting on a garment
of praise,
Embracing God and changing ways

Do people stop and listen to what you say?
As you stand offering tracks
That show them how to walk in His way?

Woman of God
I'm pleased to meet you
♥

Alipaly

Sometimes without warning my head will hurt
And my speech will falter and play tricks on me,
It literally goes all around Europe before it meets me back
in the UK!!!
But one thing I never lose
Is the ability to smile.

I claim no illness over my life,
I am made whole by the living blood of Jesus Christ.
Why do these silly episodes come and go I will never know.
But one thing for sure,
God's loving-kindness and healing power always steal the
show.

So when you hear me speak with a foreign accent
Just join me in laughter (confuse the enemy!)
Agree with me in prayer.
My joy the adversary is after,
But I decree, and I declare,
God's hands are on His daughter,
Angels surround me in the atmosphere.
My speech may be funny and sometimes not so clear,
But it never stops me from talking to my God in prayer.

So be encouraged, don't despair,
No matter what you're going through...
Reach out and touch Him for He is there.
Lean into His bosom,
Listen for His voice.
Be ready to accept Him,
He always gives us a choice.

It is not God's will when sometimes we fall ill.
So fight the good fight whilst being still.
Stop the hustle and bustle
And allow the Holy Spirit to keep vigil.

Have a blessed and glorious day
And remember,
Step back and let God have His way

The Butterfly

There's beauty in every colour
Protruding wings competing with the prettiest flower
And gentle as the princess high up in the tower

How I love the butterfly
Our lifespan is much the same
In the beginning feeling low creeping slow
Not realising the inner queen
But the magic lies in between

She stops
And transformation in a way I can't explain
Begins behind closed doors inside a cocoon
She strips
Metamorphosis has begun

For me it was because of the risen King
He broke me in the darkness
Remoulded me to wholeness
Now a vessel glorifying His righteousness

My light shines on top a hill
Where nature in its purity lies still
And out from the blooming flowers

Comes a stunning butterfly
Colours that mimic sparkling jewels
Never would you believe its small beginning
Slowly, colourless, aimlessly not sure where to go

She waits
Patiently waiting to break free
To fly high for all to see
Thank You, Lord, for creating me
For drawing out my potential
Helping me shine on top a mantle

May my life be a living testimony
One day you'll read a story
Of how this caterpillar transformed and broke free
No longer in captivity

Arms stretched out like wings
Colours forming, embracing reality
Beckoning all humanity
To let God do in you what He did in me
Let go of self, pride and vanity
Open your eyes and see
The beauty that is within

Embrace your butterfly

I will lift up my eyes to the hills— From whence comes my help? My help comes from the Lord, who made heaven and earth.

–Psalms 121:1-2

She Speaks Arise

The morning after the day before
I awake and smile at the open door
Not in my room
But a new spiritual bloom
True buds stood up and blossomed
The room was filled with their bouquet
An empowered woman spoke
Giving me something special to take away

Still, I Rise
A famous piece from Maya Angelou
Was eloquently read
As she spoke, each layer of our lives was shed
Giving glory to the Godhead

Without whom none that was spoken could have been said

She also came alive to others
Sisters, friends, daughters, cousins and mothers
Soaked in the fresh water which stirred up their gifts
And their purpose that lay dormant within

Wow, the trials and darkness we were once in,
She told how we could break out, overcome and step in...

Our Purpose was no more in doubt

The journey continues
There's more for that empowered woman to bring to you
I implore you to come and hear

Let this empowered poem
Inspire you and be encouraged to share and touch other
women too.
Believe in your own journey that's led you to THIS point...

And Still We Rise

Good Morning

The sun rises
It fights to be seen
For the clouds hover
Over the daybreak we are about to see
Waking up from sleep
Forever grateful
For many closed their eyes yesterday
And forever they will stay that way

Clearly God has a plan for you
So get up
You got things to do
Jeremiah 29:11 is a promise from Him
So don't give in to the enemy's lies
Wipe away the sleep from your eyes
Stretch, yawn, smile, sigh
And get up

Put your hand to your chest
And you feel the rhythmic beat
Give praise

Now, come on, stand
What are you going to do today?
First of all, I recommend that you pray

Thanking God for this brand-new day
As I type, the sky seems to be getting bright
You see, even the sun is beating the grey
It is winning the fight
For darkness is only meant for the night
When God says rest, it's time to sleep
So when you awake, you're energised
And then realise
God's not done with you yet

So, get up, good morning
Arise and shine
And say to yourself
The beauty of the day is mine
Yesterday was yesterday, it's done
Today is a new day, feel your power
Do not fret or be sour

You made it

Smile
Get up
Good morning

'For I know the plans and thoughts that I have for you,'
says the Lord, 'plans for peace and well-being and not
for disaster, to give you a future and a hope. Then you
will call on Me and you will come and pray to Me, and
I will hear [your voice] and I will listen to you.'

—Jeremiah 29:11-12

Arise [from spiritual depression to a new life], shine [be
radiant with the glory and brilliance of the Lord]; for
your light has come, And the glory and brilliance of the
Lord has risen upon you.

—Isaiah 60:1

Sparkle

Sparkle, like snowdrops softly falling from a moon-kissed sky,

Sparkle, like the smile in your eyes,

Sparkle, how the Spirit around your body shines,

Sparkle, like the earrings in my ears and rings on my fingers,

Sparkle, like the sun as it breaks through to a brand new day,

Just Sparkle and watch the Lord have His way.

Worth More Than Rubies

Platinum, gold, emerald and ruby
Jewels exquisite and a delight for the eyes to see
Precious stones
Yet God called a woman to be more refined

As the sunlight shines
Reflecting sparkles that dance like water under a sunset sky
Woman, thou art blessed
You were not made to be stressed
Hold your head up high and take pride in how you dress

Stand by your man as he stands by you
If you are single, stand on your own
Confident that you are looked after by the King on His throne

A woman of virtue is such a rarity in this twenty-first-century
For this is a man's desire

To find a wife more precious than sapphire, silver or gold
Her beauty lies within her
Dare I say, more precious than the largest ruby to behold

This is what God delights in
A woman filled with riches and honour

A woman of peace
A woman of wisdom
A woman of splendour
A woman who has a path set to get to God's Kingdom
Are you that woman?

Are you called blessed?
Or are you falling short eating the words of idleness?
Can a man trust you as his wife?
Can you seal your lips so as not to cause strife?
Who oh who can find a virtuous wife?

I pray Proverbs 31:10-12
will be your claim to fame

⁓⁓

*Who can find a virtuous wife? For her worth is far
above rubies. The heart of her husband safely trusts
her; So he will have no lack of gain. She does him good
and not evil All the days of her life.*

—Proverbs 31:10-12

⁓⁓

4

RELATIONSHIP
BREAKDOWN

Clipped Wings of a Butterfly

To me, marriage is a gift from God, and I respect it so much—so you could imagine my heartache when mine ended the first time. We blew it. We were inexperienced and had no godly support or advice, as we were not practicing Christians. Ours was a rollercoaster of being truly in love and arguments that turned into physical fights.

After I became very sick, things got worse, and sadly, it all came to an end.

Six years later, I met and fell in love with a man who became my second husband. Soon after we were married, things changed, and over seven long years of being abused in so many hurtful ways possible, this marriage, too, came to a bitter end.

I was left withdrawn, emotionally, spiritually and mentally broken. If it wasn't for God, my best friend and the love and support from my siblings, I would have become a woman scorned with bitterness and hatred towards God and man. I was in a well of deception from the enemy's whispering in my ears, 'How could your so-called God be called your Father? How could He let these bad things happen to you? He doesn't care for you, doesn't love you…' and so the voices kept on.

With now two failed marriages, I said to myself all men were the same, and I hated them.

Well, praise God, my Redeemer lives. He cares, He loves, He never gives up on us. He took me from that tormenting well, placed His arms around me, soothed and repaired my heart and transformed my mind to conform to His. No, not all men are the same. Looking back, I see where God tried to warn me against the second marriage, but He also gives us free will, and I blindly kept following my will and ignoring His. A word to the wise: not every hiccup you face is from the devil! Sometimes, it may be God trying to save your behind.

The one good thing that came out of that broken place is that I had many moments with the Lord, times of talking and then listening, expressing and releasing all my pain, hope and expectations on paper. As I wrote my poems, the healing began inside. I also realised that as I shared my testimony in groups and wrote poems that surfaced from within that dry place, women were witnessed, too. Many have approached me to say they are or have been in abusive marriages or relationships unable to escape.

My testimony and poems gave them the light they needed in their own darkness, seeing me stand in the grace of God, upright in His strength, smiling with the fullness of His joy that cannot be taken away.

What follows are some of the poems written during that winter season of my life, which turned to autumn, blossomed into spring and bloomed into summer.

Wedding Day

(Poem to my Fiancé)

Being born-again meant I was starting a new life
So much was stolen, I didn't know how to live again
Every day struggling through, constantly waiting for a
breakthrough
Then, my darling, I met you
You became the silver lining in my clouds
Loving you made me proud

The first day I saw you, I was just passing by chance
And there you were, sitting in front of your house
A conversation started; a friendship grew.
Walking together in the early evening sun
Talking, laughing and sharing our testimonies
We soon realised we were each other's destiny

Since we met, my past has been easier to forget
Sharing in your company, your life has become a part of me
The trials we've been through shouldn't be a regret
But a learning tool to use in our future, which God has set

I have learned in my nine years of being born again
Through spoken words of wisdom
Testimonies of God's Kingdom people

Sermons by pastors, in sadness and in laughter
I understand what it is to have agape love
And my life's ambition is to be a virtuous wife you'd be proud of

Today you have made me the happiest woman
From the moment I said, 'I do,' that was it; I belonged only to you
Yes, my love, you have made my life complete
I have always dreamt of having lots of children
So when I had my five, I thought I had accomplished my desire
But God had a greater number in mind,
And gave me four more; now I'm blessed with nine

Our children are truly a blessing to us
Their questions, hopes and dreams for the future keep us focused
Every decision we make from now on
Will be done to enhance their footsteps to a higher level
Let us never forget God's hand in all of this
His loving tender mercies
Have brought us through every crisis
From this day on, you and I and our children shall walk as one
With Jesus, the light to our feet, Jehovah Jireh, our Prince of Peace,
I believe we will never face defeat

The Great Divide

It's so one-sided and frustrating
Two separate families came together as one
But there is still an unseen separation
And something must be done

Why, when my son doesn't, the big man's face swell
And shouting, flip sake, how much more can he tell?
But when his daughter doesn't do what she ought
He's bawling at me to shut meh mout

I have never seen his children wake up and straightaway
brush their teeth
But when my little ones say they want to eat
He tells them. 'What kind of example was set?
Yuh mean yuh ain't wash yuh mout yet?'

'Everyone, wash and put away your own clothes.'
But as ever, one person (me) ends up folding all man's
clothes
'Complain?' he says. 'Do as I do and leave it right there'
Yet if I do, the pile will not clear

In the earlies when he came to visit
The moans and groans at the sight of dirty clothes

Telling me 'This won't do, fix these kids before I marry you'
But I tell you, now that we've tied the knot
Things are not quite correct in the boulevard
Their clothes constantly taking residence on the chair
Everyone just walking pass
Nowhere to sit
As far as everyone's concerned, they've done their bit
Ah telling yuh, this is real sh**

Why when my children mess up, he has all the right to moan
But when his children do the same,
I'm told to leave them alone, don't call no-one's name
Or in front of them he'll put me to shame
Yet I still feel so ashamed, I shame, I shame, I shame
This is not lifting Jesus' name
How can we stand in church on a Sunday,
Lifting our hands to proclaim the power of His love?
Something must be done, 'cuz this is not glorifying God
Somehow, this marriage needs to turn full circle
Husband, wife and children
We sure need a miracle
I surrender my ring to my Heavenly King
To him, through all this, I shall not stop worshipping
I open the door and welcome Him in
And drive out the narcissistic enemy in my husband's heart
Give us, Lord, a brand new start.

Mountain Top Experience

I'm feeling tired inside
So broken my pride I can't hide
And I'm wondering where my journey is going.

I'm trying not to curl up and hide
My future rolls like a turbulent ride
And I'm wondering where my journey is going.

Surely God's by my side
Holding me close as He guides
Because He loves me sincerely
While I'm wondering where my journey is going.

Can't speak, can't tell you how I feel
Not openly, so afraid to be real
I'm climbing a mountain, and the journey is hurting.

Show me, collapsed down on my knees
Tears flowing as my Spirit intercedes
And I praise you and give you all the glory.

Magnify
Glorify
Shout on high, with my palms raised to the sky

My load falls as I harken to your call
I wait for your answer
Stop feeling like a failure
You're the light in my darkness
I'm coming out of the wilderness

On top of the mountain,
I can see clearly where my journey has taken me.
Hallelujah,
Glory be to the one true God Jesus who rescued me
And I see clearly where my journey has taken me
Hallelujah, Glory be to the one true God Jesus who rescued me
And I see clearly where my journey has taken me
Hallelujah,
Glory be to the one true God, Jesus who stripped me free
And I see clearly where my journey has taken
me...

Up the mountain,
He set me free
Hallelujah God favoured me.
Amen

Fly High

Fly high, but I won't reach the sky if I die
Sometimes, life can feel like a slow death
You feel yourself slipping away daily
Contemplating if it would be easier to speed up the process
But with what reward? What success?
Is this the result of stress?
Is this all the hurts compressed?
Packed so tight like sardines in a tin,
Is it too late for the King of Kings to step in?

My chest is tight, tears stifled, stomach in knots, I can't digest
A lump in my breast…
Worse than cancer, it will quicker put me in a hearse
I can't shout, can't have an outburst
It just gets worse
Atmosphere so overwhelming all I can do is cry
Silent tears of despair
Tears for a love that refuses to repair
Our sweet union he rejects to share

Who is out there to hear my thoughts?
All the words and feelings I cannot say out loud
If I do, then all would know…

That my marriage and vows were untrue, fabricated
Who would believe the devil would/could be so sly?
In the twinkling of an eye,
As subtle as the soft evening breeze,
That he would move into our relationship
And cause such an outbreak

Worse than sores of a leper
Worse than a crusty, hardened wart
Worse than a battle I have ever fought
I didn't know his love for me would be so short.

Jesus, what do I do?
I gave my life to him but first to You
Can You not forgive me for where I've gone wrong?
Is this punishment for things left undone?
My heart feels like a million lines of cracks runs through it
And if I breathe too hard, it will eventually fall apart

Jesus, be my friend, my support, my guide
For this pain is hard to hide
I need You so desperately
I have tried to plead in prayer
But the words I cannot find
I feel so blind
I can't see the end
The end to the pain
The end to the strain
The end to the shame

Jesus, I call upon Your name
For Your sovereign hand to rest upon our lives
And our lost love to be revived
Take my life, yes, I want to die
But I know if I do, my eternity will not be with you
So, in Your time, Lord, I shall fly high
And meet You in the sky

Love suffers long and is kind; love does not envy;
love does not parade itself, is not puffed up;
does not behave rudely, does not seek its own,
is not provoked, thinks no evil; does not rejoice
in iniquity, but rejoices in the truth; bears all things,
believes all things, hopes all things, endures all things.

−1 Corinthians 13:4-7

From Truth to Pretend

I know you
Yes, you...you are me
For we share the same journey
But shall speak an individual testimony

We married young
The fairytale stories were sold
As the finger was dressed in a band of gold
No warning of calamities was ever told
The princess has her prince
A new family as two become one
God in His divinity
Blessed your union for eternity

What happened?
When did the fairy tale change its end?
How did we get from truth to pretend?
Act fast, don't hesitate
For it is never too late
God says He'll walk with us, so step forward, don't hesitate

Don't worry, says the Lord

I clothed the flowers, remember?
And look how they display their colours with splendour

Render your garments, jewellery and hearts of gold
Watch how I, your Lord & Saviour
Will take every bad thing and make it a great love story
that's ever to be told

You said, 'I do.' He said, 'I promise to
I submit...and I will love you
Let's both commit
And work as one not two
Lord, we walk and follow You'

Then the door opened, and the enemy crept in
Pressures of life causing cracks within
Burdens on shoulders
Monetary responsibilities had the loudest say
The start of marital strife
He sees black
She sees grey
No one is seeing the Light shining the way

He sees the grass greener on the other side
His water hoses the devil hides
Wife's petals are drying, her lawn has gone brown as hay
She speaks to no one as she is riddled with pride
The devil laughs as he conjures isolation
And hour by hour, day by day
Devastation is coming in to stay

Wait...
Come to stay, you say?
No no no
There is work to be done
The woman reading this is Proverbs 21
She knows how to pray
Her spirit intercedes what her tongue can't say
She goes to the gate
She threshes the floors
And cries out to God
'TELL THAT JEZEBEL NO MORE NO MORE'
Her tantalising is against the law
Don't be fooled by the tears of his wife
God gave her a husband
And the vow declared it was for life
Her tears are her strength and she's ready to fight

Jesus is the Truth the Way and the Light
Yes, it is He whose light shines so bright
Trust even if you cannot bear the weight that stifles you
in the night
As the tears fall on an empty pillow
Where your husband rested his head after he kissed you
goodnight

God says not long now
Keep fighting the fight
Await the breakthrough
Your husband will soon see My light

And run from that woman who used him for delight
He shall scorn her touch and lust not for her ways
But long for his wife as he kneels, he prays...

'God, God forgive me for I strayed
I failed and forgot in whose arms I belong'

And my actions have been of a rebellious husband
Set me free from the jezebel's captivity
Forgive me, Lord, and tell my wife for me...
I'm coming home
I've been under attack
Please forgive me
Please take me back
Let's share our forever
As we vowed together
For better for worse
For richer for poorer
As long as we put our Father first
We will overcome the enemy
And live out our vows
Verse by verse
Forever

Wounded Wife Wins

Oh, the love of Christ surrounds our lives.
Captured like the sweet essence of spring.
Catapulting my heartstrings and churning on my soul within.
The beauty of the love you hold, how you speak of it so bold...I see your love will never grow old, captured in the essence of spring.

Me... a wounded wife who was broken bruised and torn, abused as if I were the subject of porn.
I looked over unto the freshly mowed lawn
And thought if only the landscape would cry out for me at dawn.
For when the sun awakes and the flowers partake in a dance, My spirit within also wakes out of a trance...

And then my eyes open as I drop the last tear,
I hear Christ whisper gently in my ear
'Fear not, My child, I am here. My love for you is greater, so beloved, do not fear. You too will experience love, not just from Me but your significant other. His love for you will shine through and together, you will deal with the scars.'

The lawn I see is the Gardens of Gethsemane, where lovers dance and heart palpitate at a glimpse of their spouse's glance.

Oh, I pray God opens the gate for me to enter once more, And my heart will beat for my husband whilst my soul magnifies the Lord within...

And then...

Yes, then...

This wounded wife shall win.

The Wife in Need of Interception...

Strengthen my heart when it's weak
Let my heart sing when I have no voice to speak
Help me to zip my lip!
For when it opens in anger, it often rocks the ship.

Conform my mind
save me from going blind
Break me, melt me, rearrange me
shake off the enemy from my back
the way he is saddling me, you'd think I signed a contract!

I'm no puppet, devil can't move me
Greater is he within me than he that is in the world
I will never sell my soul over, even if he offered PURE
gold.
Living this life everyday
God doesn't give a spirit of fear, help us to share in prayer.

Unify us to make us strong
Unveil the living word so he sees and knows the truth
Jesus is the Risen Son who bared many wounds on Calvary
So, we could inherit salvation and be free

Take away the heaviness that cloaks this house
cover us instead with love and make us as one
Help my vows not be a lie, let me fulfil my duties as wife
and mother
may my past be a positive testimony to help every single
mother (and other)!

Surely, my family will make it
Every lie from the enemy will be shattered
every demon that tried to shake us down scattered
Honour and Glory to you, our King, who washed us clean
with His blood
and cast our sins in the sea of forgetfulness

In Jesus' name, my spouse shall have spiritual growth and
start to believe he was born to live and not die
and that the vows he made were not a hoax, and realise
the devil had him living a lie

Those who have ears, let them hear
and take this new knowledge and cover us in prayer!

Work of Art

An unspoken word within the sketch
Smiles that speak indifference to what's portrayed
Somewhat heartbroken
An observer would sense

They pose trying hard not to disclose
A relationship that's lost its scent of a sweet English rose
Where is the sparkle in her eyes?
His smile seems like a continuous sigh
A love that once was on Cloud Nine
Has now fallen, sleeping dormant it lies

The artist takes another stencil
Trying to expose joy as they sit still
Just then, the man's hand rises to her shoulder
He squeezes it softly
His smile now speaks openly
Of the love he still holds for her deeply
The pressures of life knocked them unsteady

But their love struggles to be revived
For in their hearts,
It still beats alive.

Remembrance

The air was humid
And the mockingbirds sang
The time when you took my hand
And declared you loved me and would to the end

To the end…

The times my heartbeat increased when you entered the room
And my speech quivered
Because I could not hide my smile.
The warmth of your touch
And you promised me then
You'd love me to the end of time

To the end of time…

The walks and talks
And the outings to restaurants so fine.
The annual Christmas dinners hosted by your employer
Where we danced and joked
You held me and introduced me proudly as your lady of
all time

Of all time…

The engagement, the wedding planning
All the gifts and promises
The moment we stood up together
With all our children in unity
And declared
'This is our family for all eternity'

All eternity…

The flight, the honeymoon
The beach, the sun, the love
The local food.
And the boat ride on our return
You held my hand, no turning back

The front door opened, 'Kids, we're back'
And our life started
'It' started, 'It' moved in

It started
It moved in…

The first time you turned in response and snapped at me
And I jumped startled
Hairs rose on the back of my neck
That frightful feeling

Then talked myself around
'It's okay, it's all okay'
And then nearly every day 'it' came back
'It' was here to stay

Here to stay...

The arguments, the crying
The fights, the shouting
Thinking it needs to stop
'It' needs to die
The more I prayed the more 'it' attacked
The bickering, the bitterness
The resentment, the lies
The hate just escalated

The hate just escalated...

The brokenness, the mess, the stress
And not knowing how to stop what so early on began
The tears, the fears,
The unawares
And the sun goes up and the sun goes down

Remembering the time there was no frown when you said
my name
Remembering when you said you would love me to the
end of time

Realising now that your time and God's time was not the
same
Will 'it' ever go away?
Will you ever take me back to that day I remember?
The 5th of September
As you placed the gold band on my finger
And in front of God and witnesses
Vowed to me 'I do'
Promising to love me to the end of time

The end of time…

Remember?

The Truth Shall Set You Free Unconditionally

Are you there?
Are you aware?
Your Creator has placed in you a gift to inspire,

Chosen by God,
Created in His image.
A woman of divine purpose; a reflection of His love for you.

Do you know your worth?
Or have the lies of the enemy blinded your eyes?

Are you wearing a mask enclosed in pain?
Walking around feeling downcast and shame?
Rise up, my daughters,
I beckon you to the Truth.

Truth... so powerful is this word as it rolls of the tongue,
It has the characteristics of a French romantic!
God loves you, my daughter,
He brings you Truth to wash away the lies.

He facilitates your steps
He is opening the doors... Forget your flaws,
Forget the negative words that have been said,
Covering you, saturated you, and left you for dead.

Believe in His Truth

The words of the Godhead... Spirit led you were brought
here to this page.
Be inspired and let Truth make a way.
Be inspired, my daughters,
Your purpose is revealed today.

Peace I leave with you, My peace I give to you; not as the world gives do I give to you. Let not your heart be troubled, neither let it be afraid.

–John 14:27

5

JOY OF THE LORD

First it was Fragrance

An aroma I could not remember
Was this a scent I knew from before,
A battle from yesteryear's seeping through an open door?

How did I unlock the door without a visible key?
I go on bended knee, asking God to cover me
And as single flowers come together to form a bouquet
God raised me up with His hands
Supporting me by my outstretched arms
And the heat of His love filled the atmosphere
There was a shift... it will be okay

First it was fragrance
Then it turned to fire
I rose and danced
And danced on the devil, the chief liar

I stepped to the left
Did the electric slide to the right
Stood up straight and stamped
There was a melody in the air

Angels singing
I heard them clear

There was a fresh aroma
It was the fragrance of my worship

I twirled like a ballerina
Moved my feet like a dancer in the Irish Riverdance
Worshipping nonstop till there were beads of sweat
Yet the fire still burned
The hinges of the door melted in the heat
The enemy had no choice but to accept defeat

First it was fragrance
Then it turned to fire
My worship is my weapon
This is how I win my battles

This is how you win win win
Stifle your problems, your battles,
with the smoke of your worship...

Dance

Choose to Be...

Anything, exceptionally,
Unapologetically you
Choose to be someone with purpose
Walking into your destiny
Greeting those you pass by amicably

Choose to be...
Free,
Basking in a field of fragrance
Entwined in between colourful flowers in a spiritual dance
This pathway is not by chance
Step by step, your faith shall be enhanced

On a cloudy day there is always light
In the stillness of night, the stars in unison shine bright

The clouds choose...
Hold the water or rain?
Gather together or separate?
So, what's your choice?

Hold onto your gifts and talents?

Or shower the world touching hundreds and thousands of women and men
Opening up their eyes to God's plans for them
Enriching lives, abandoning lies,
Allowing the Spirit of God to flow, marking the steps for you to go
Spreading the gospel in His apparel
Opening eyes with words concise
Bringing truth of the ultimate sacrifice

I choose life
I choose it abundantly
I choose to laugh
I choose to dance
I choose to let my secret known
Who makes me this way?
Why do I smile through my eyes
The tears clothed in diamonds sparkling like a trillion stars
My life, wow,
My grin stretches; my colourful hair swept to the side as I disclose...

I chose Jesus, but He first chose me.
And after 1001 testimonies of all He's done for me

I choose to be joyful,
He chose me to be free.

Transition

Help me breathe, help me take control
All around me is riddled by senseless sin
Why can't I hold within
The beauty of Your love?

Why can't the dove of peace be in my easy reach?
My life in turmoil, I sit still,
Closing my eyes
I see colours swirling like sunrays on a sunset on a beach
One day, yes one day my story will be used to teach

Pain has taken over, grabbed a hold...
It's so bold
Right now, I feel nothing around my peers
I just don't fit in; this is not where I belong

You lent out Your hand and took me as Your bride
You love and look after me,
Stripped me of pride

Old acquaintances are like bitterness in attack
My tongue is armoured ready to strike back
But wait,

Stop, You say, don't let the enemy snatch the glory and
have his way
March to his camp and claim alimony
Let him pay back what he stole, and wave the victory flag
of your testimony

Help me breathe
Help me stay in control
My body and mind are frail from within
My soul feels like it's about to cave in
How, oh Lord, do I tell them they are living in sin?
I take notes, but end up tearing them up and filling the bin

New friends in the faith become my next of kin
They become my intercessors and support

They stand with me through every battle that's been fought
It was a fight and I got injured
Heart broken
Lungs deflated
Kidneys dehydrated
Stomach shook
Ribs cracked
Bones chipped
Eyes sunken
Nose stuffed
Ears blocked

Spirit shattered
Mouth sealed but I was able to cry out...

Spirit of the living Lord fall afresh on me
Break me
Melt me
Mould me
Fill me
Take me

Jesus took control and made me whole
The Author of my life
Healer of my soul
Amen.

Transition: the process or a period of changing from one state or condition to another.

It's All About Faith

Here I am
Sitting in a warped mind of confusion
Thinking of all things
What could've, would've, should've but didn't happen to
my family

Shutting down
My mind in a world of thoughts
Thoughts so jumbled, no sense comes from them
Sitting down and the fog surrounds me
Rising from the depths of the earth
And from the sky above
The stars and universe sparkle
How easy it seems, when in trouble
You forget about God's love

You want to smile but it's not there
My heart is turbulent with despair
In the back of my mind, I hear a shout
'God cares, my lovely, have no doubt'

I know He sees me
I know He knows me
I know, when I look back with my Lord
And I pinpoint times when I've been low

I'm sure I'll envision a parent
Lovingly cradling His child

Oh, gentle Jesus, meek and mild
Don't let the devil take a hold of me and mines
Teach me to cope when times are hard
Through my prayers I shall see miracles, wonders and signs

It's all about faith
So I shall continue to pray when things don't go my way
I love you, Lord, may it show throughout each day
I desire the best for my family
It is frustrating to see them not listening to what can set them free
Extended family filled with cracks and disharmony
With the Trinity I know they can make it
I shall get up from sitting and in the gap, I will stand
For no matter what may come our way
I know their lives are in Your hands

I love the Lord, because He has heard
My voice and my supplications.
² Because He has inclined His ear to me,
Therefore I will call upon Him as long as I live.
³ The pains of death surrounded me,
And the pangs of Sheol laid hold of me;
I found trouble and sorrow.
⁴ Then I called upon the name of the Lord:
'O Lord, I implore You, deliver my soul!'
⁵ Gracious is the Lord, and righteous;
Yes, our God is merciful.
⁶ The Lord preserves the simple;
I was brought low, and He saved me.
⁷ Return to your rest, O my soul,
For the Lord has dealt bountifully with you.
⁸ For You have delivered my soul from death,
My eyes from tears,
And my feet from falling.
⁹ I will walk before the Lord
In the land of the living.
I believed; therefore I spoke,
'I am greatly afflicted.'

¹¹ *I said in my haste,*
"All men are liars."
¹² *What shall I render to the Lord*
For all His benefits toward me?
¹³ *I will take up the cup of salvation,*
And call upon the name of the Lord.
¹⁴ *I will pay my vows to the Lord*
Now in the presence of all His people.
¹⁵ *Precious in the sight of the Lord*
Is the death of His saints.

¹⁶ *O Lord, truly I am Your servant;*
I am Your servant, the son of Your maidservant.
You have loosed my bonds.
¹⁷ *I will offer to You the sacrifice of thanksgiving,*
And will call upon the name of the Lord.
¹⁸ *I will pay my vows to the Lord*
Now in the presence of all His people,
¹⁹ *In the courts of the Lord's house,*
In the midst of you, O Jerusalem.

Praise the Lord!

—Psalm 116:1-19

I'm Free

Set your spirit free
Don't let it suffocate in captivity
Let loose the bondage that stifles your soul
Come unto Jesus and he'll make you whole
Break away from the clutches of sin
It's tearing you down
Making you frown
Take a deep breath
Slowly exhale
Now let Jesus take control, He'll never fail

Dry the tears from your eyes, my sweet little child
Cast your fears away
And look forward to another day
When you wake up at the break of dawn
Do not do another thing
But pray, lay a hold of God
And thank Him for this brand-new day
For you are living on borrowed time
So you need to give God thanks and praise
And let Him guide you in all of your ways

He sees your tears, knows your fears
He knows your needs, hears your plea...
Free me, Lord, free me from this misery

I can't take no more of this heavy load
I know You will not give me more than I could bear
Lord, I have lost weight from the last time You weighed me
I don't think much more I can carry

Oh, my child, have you such little faith?
Do you not remember I know the number of hairs on your head?
Of every minute, hour, day of your life?
I know beforehand when you'd meet trouble and strife
I also knew you would be born-again before you could comprehend
With Me in your life there is always a brighter tomorrow
I'll lead you out of pain and sorrow
It's not about the weight loss you mentioned before
My precious child, this is a spiritual war
The devil will try to steal to the end
Even though he will lose, he likes to play 'let's' pretend'
Just lean on Me when you are feeling low
Trust in Me let me set the flow
Talk to me in prayer
And let our relationship grow
Through every trial you will get stronger
And they will come a time satan can touch you no longer
You see there is a reason for every season

But you are blood washed by Me,
I set your spirit free
Cast away your burdens and come closer, lean on My shoulder
Now this is your season to fight a good fight and finish your race
Until one day we'll meet face to face

No longer bound
You are free

6

DEALING WITH GRIEF
AND LOSS

Christopher Curtis Anderson Ryan
1961-2012

I sat looking at the screen of my laptop for a good hour, closed it and re-opened it two days later. Why? I just didn't know where to begin in regards to bringing up the subject of my brother. My thoughts examined many different avenues—our childhood, my siblings in general, our lives, our upbringing—but truly, I was stuck. How could I possibly describe the love, his character, what made us laugh, what made us annoyed with him? How could I possibly convey the uttermost grief we suffered at his untimely death, the tears, the suffocating loss?

There simply wasn't a way at all. I decided the only way forward was to just start typing and see how God would knit each letter into words that then linked into sentences. It was a hard one.

I smiled as I came to realise that all the above was woven into the poems written around the anniversaries of his death and acknowledging his birthday each year. The magnitude of how we love and miss him is found within these verses. My heart warms as I smile, thinking how on earth is it possible that I find new things to say each passing year.

My brother was affectionately known as Chris or Andy, depending what hit your tongue first. Out of all my living siblings, he was the fifth eldest. Such a happy soul who always found a way to cheer you up. He was an awesome big brother, eight years older than me. He always gave me pocket money as a child and great advice when I became an adult.

You know what? I'm just going to share with you all the poems made in his name, and I guarantee you will get the essence of the love. One thing I am happy about is our love for one another was shown in his living years. Remember to tell your family how much you love them so they know it. Don't wait until they've gone and your words are just said in sympathy cards.

Someone has stolen my priceless jewel; I just want it back. It was a rare jewel that made me laugh made me mad and made me think outside of the box! I just want it back. My heart feels as if it will stop beating, the tears never ceasing and the feeling to scream increasing. I just want my big brother back. Sleep is like a stranger; the nights are so long and the days drift by so slow. My jewel is gone. Why? I'll never know.

Death, Where Is Thy Sting?

I'm captivated by the essence of spring
Since my big brother's passing
It has become intoxicating
The light breeze tickles my nose
The sweet scents of tulips, daffodils and roses
Like a tree, I await to be awoken from winter's sleep
My body and soul feel liked cracked branches
Undertaken not a cold season
But a death without reason

We've been left standing
Stripped naked and laid bare for the sting of death to tear
But in time, I know that within the cracks, the buds will
soon appear
As evergreens.
My family Andy left behind will stand in full attire
Dancing in memory of the son, brother, brother-in-law,
father, grandfather, father-in-law, nephew, uncle, cousin,
lover, companion and friend… so abruptly taken
Let us dance, but remember, walk life's road with caution,
for we too are targeted to receive death's portion!

Downcast with grief, I try to stand proud, dressed loud
Sprayed with the multi-colours of the colourful soul of Andy

In this fiercest storm of emotions, tossing me, bending me,
trying to break me
I shall—we shall—rise like a ballerina in the climax of a
heart-pounding play
Still able to hold the pose when she rises to dance on her toes
With grace, with beauty, with elegance and firm unwavering
position

Just like the evergreen rooted firm in a solid foundation—
Our foundation needs to be Christ our Lord and Saviour
So through every weather storm of death, trial and
tribulation
Our trust, hope and faith in Jesus shall see us through
God knew my brother
God knows you
We are not exempt from this path

One day I was crippled with tears, bawling as I remembered
the sight of my brother lying lifeless on the cold wooden floor
And the pain that pierced me was that he was all alone…
Suddenly I envisioned someone kneeling quietly and
affectionately at his side
I watched as I pictured the light of day and night passing
twice
The vision of this mystery person stayed by his side
And disappeared the moment Cousin Jane arrived
So this—
The peace my Heavenly Father gave to me, I unselfishly
share with you

That my brother wasn't alone
An angel came and kept him company
To God be the glory
Our ever-present Friend to the end.

Gone But Not Forgotten

(Two years after)

Rain doesn't make this day easier
Memories sore in and my gut starts a-churning
Just a normal Good Friday 2 yrs. ago today…

Got up went to walk and pray, sung praises and hallelujahs
and so begun my day.
Bid farewell to my church family as I had to rush off home
and look forward to my day,
You see, all the family was coming over and cooking was
on the way.
Big sis had already arrived by the time I got in… so there we
were, cooking, chatting, laughing and giggling and waiting
for the rest of our tribe to fall in… and have a great fish day.
The phone rings, my big sis picks up
Hello...
Laughter stops

'WHAT YOU TELLING ME' She's shouting 'SHUT UP
SHUT UP'
All cooking stops
She screams, she screams she screeeeeeeams
She drops.

The air thickens. I can't breathe. I fall to my knees. I can't get up.

I manage to dial. I hear her voice… 'SANDRAAAA MY BROTHER DEAD'

She comes within mins, takes the kids

I'm in the car, Brother-in-law Pete driving us far

I don't see traffic, don't see people, don't hear conversation, can't hear thoughts…

Husband whispering words of comfort but only my spirit hears for I am STILL

We reach… I fall out the car, someone holding me back…'Leh me go'… Ah seein' meh brother lying down flat… 'Leh me go'

We came, my sweet bro, we kissed you goodbye, and gently, carefully closed your eyes, We touched your face and your hands we embraced. So cold… So bloody cold…

But within me today is warmth. Knowing you are with the angels and giggling how they must be watching your dance moves… I hear you explaining to them that you're stepping to their lyrics of praise and not the musical instruments, which is the normal way!

I try, bro, to do as you did… follow up on family and friends, the distant ones, but, Bwoy, I realised there is only

ONE you and even though I try, Andy, boy, ah can't fit into your shoes...

I'm not giving up, I still put the creds in my phone and randomly pick who to phone. I feel their smile through the line as I know that they are happy to hear a Ryan's voice even if it's not your own.

Nuh worry yourself, bro, I still watching out for your girl, call her from time to time and invite her around to dine at mine... Jane's doing fine

Words can't express how much I miss you. Mum tells me off because I can't let go... 'Oh gosh, Ali,' she says, 'leh de boy rest, when yuh gone let go?' To that I don't know
Weaning has begun, ashes gone to Kell's, no longer with me, hun. August coming... Oh Lord, let's not talk about dat one!!

So today I shall lift my Spirits and do what you did best... find a nice bottle of champers and toast you, your life, your memories, your words of wisdom, your advice, your smile... Your love and happiness.

You spoke words of life into my marriage when many others (including myself) spoke death. Your words we shall not let them go. Thank you for embracing Michael. He loves you so much for doing so.

One of a kind, my brother...

Andy, gonna go now and try to get through this day.
Nice talking to you in this way
Reminiscing about that awful day is not the best way,
I can't control the thoughts that flow in like waves
Memories of you calm the heartbeat, memories of your happy feet...
I love you; I love you; I love You... I miss you I do, I do, I do...

Rest In Eternal Peace, Bro xxxx

Happy Birthday

(Three years on)

Another birthday
Another year we cannot share
The day arrives
But your age stays the same
The month where you were first, and I am the last
Three years have passed
And I still must ask
Why oh why were you taken so fast?

I see you daily when I pick up my phone
Constantly reminding myself God said, 'He was NOT alone
And take comfort in knowing he is seated by My throne'
(I guess this is when you take a breather from dancing with the angels all day long!)
Family sighing saying, 'It is time to let go'
After all, we paid big money travelling to Trinidad for our final goodbye.

I hold on to childhood days
Holding on to your loving ways
As a child, you gave me newspapers to read

You said the papers would teach me more about the world
than the children's storybooks I read.
Why oh why didn't I call you that fatal week? Just to check
in—I might have noticed you were feeling sick and weak

I lovingly think back when you got your first paid job
On your payday, you never forgot me
Slipped me a fiver and said spend it wisely
As a little girl, your baby sis,
This opportunity to bless me you never missed
Five pounds back in the day made a child's eye shine with
delight
Awwww, do you remember, bro, how we used to go and
fly kites?
Losing you so suddenly, the pain is worse than a ruptured cyst
Why oh why do we have to experience pain like this?

But hey hey hey...
Today would've been your 54th birthday
And knowing you, you would be having a Champaign
breakfast to start celebrating your day
I have been preparing myself all last week...
Did my nails, did my hair with colours to brighten away
any sadness that tried to peak
I laughed all weekend and celebrated life in remembrance
of you
I thought of that saying, 'Start as you mean to go on!'
And that way, by the time this day came, I'd be so happy I
wouldn't shed a tear

Well the sun is shining, I said a prayer and sang a song or two
My heart is mildly heavy, but I think the sting of grief is not as strong
I think my tactics surely won

Today I smile
Today I dance
Today I cast aside the cares of this world
Today I embrace all the blessings our Heavenly Father has graced me with
Today I give thanks and praise
For a brother that shared some of my best days
And was a blessing to me throughout my forty-odd years
Why oh why you had to go?
The answer is I'll never know, but what is true and will never change
Is my love for you, bro, it will forever stay the same

Yes, gone too soon
But this day, the 1st of June
I smile and give thanks as I say to you...

HAPPY BIRTHDAY

＊ ＊

My soul melts from heaviness;
Strengthen me according to Your word

—Psalm 119:28

Fear not, for I am with you;
Be not dismayed, for I am your God.
I will strengthen you,
Yes, I will help you,
I will uphold you with My righteous right hand.

—Isaiah 41:10

Blessed be the God and Father of our Lord Jesus
Christ, the Father of mercies and God of all comfort

—2 Corinthians 1:3

＊ ＊

Through the Lord's mercies we are not consumed,
Because His compassions fail not.
They are new every morning;
Great is Your faithfulness.

—Lamentations 3:22-23

Most assuredly, I say to you that you will weep and
lament, but the world will rejoice; and you will be
sorrowful, but your sorrow will be turned into joy.

—John 16:20

June's First Day

That month always sung a merry tune
Summer always seemed to begin in June
Us Ryans ruled...
You were the first and I the last
Like the towers of a castle's wall,
You at the beginning and I at the end
I laugh behind a smile as I struggle for my mind to still
pretend.
That this silly nightmare with you gone will surely end
And I can dance even until the music is no more
My feet flapping like a delicate butterfly with beauty
and grace
At an airy Riverdance's pace
I smile and spin, searching for your face just so when
I stop I know where to run and embrace...to leap with
joy and say as I catch my breath...

'We're here, bro, we're at June's gate!
Happy Birthday, my lovely'...
Hold hands crisscross, spin look up to a sunshine sky
See the clouds puffed up with patches of blue, clear blue
Then I open my eyes, yes opened my eyes and realised
it was imagined

I imagined you

Dancing with me sipping Champagne at breakfast, hearing the birds sing Happy June Happy Birthday to the first...

But June's door stands open, the door swings, no-one's there.
One of the castle's towers is unoccupied

Patches of clear blue on a puffed-up pillow where I cried...
I take a breath
I exhale
I look at your picture on the side of my wall
Your smile so electrifying it sparks my heart
I hear life around me making such a noise...
Life of a flock of robins chirping merrily
The chorus line needs a standing ovation
Such tiny birds but their sound brings jubilation
How fitting for Robin to come and sing at the foot of my door, watched me and took flight... I just knew that little bird came to say you are all right.

So, I step in...
Hello June,
It's not the same
My other end isn't there...

I liked it when you were the beginning and I the end, you the first and I the last
How time has passed... just five years but it's gone by so fast

For you, my brother, I shall sing a merry tune
And thank God that the 1st of June always belongs to you
For me my summer begins today and in 29 days it will be my birthday sealing June up and placing this month in my heart box!

The sweet breeze and calmness of this morning, silent prayers and I smile in appreciation that I, yes I, was your... still am your baby sis and you, big brother, I will always miss

I send a kiss to heaven's gate, and I know it shall permeate, seep through till it finds you at the music/dance floor station (yes there is such a place... God of all creation made it for my bro so he could praise dance to the lyrics!!)

Such an overcast sky I look up and wonder why, and my smile turns to a giggle and my giggle to watery-eyed laughter, as I imagine the clouds are closed curtains as we did in our house parties years and years before

If I hear thunder today, I know it'll be your feet on the dance floor...

Yay Heaven ah Tun up today

Time is a Healer

(Seven years on)

They say time makes things easier
That it lets open wounds find closure
But the same time shows itself each year
And unknowingly from my eyes fall a tear
Because time cannot replace a loved one you hold dear
Don't get me wrong, the sting has gone
It's those times we meet to have a lime
Chatter, kicks and laughter
Then we gather after...
Come come, my brothers my sister
Let's take a picture
And at that point the thoughts begin
I smile, say cheese
But a knife cuts within... there is one missing
Oh, my dayzzz your joy and laughter
Miss your dancing
The sound of your voice
When in agreement says 'Ent' and shout your favourite
'Yeah Yeah'
Aww man, Chris
Today marks the day
You left this earth

Spoke your last word
Yet the sun shines
It's warm
Then...
The breeze blows cold and harder
Blossoms and rain fall
Like mixed emotions I have inside
I find comfort in The Father
Looking at your pictures
Giggling at some shots
Some of them you look absolutely crazy
Some of you dancing, liming and smiling
Some events I didn't remember and totally forgot.

You my brother
Are embedded in my memory
In my heart
In my soul
You will never get old
The same face
The same smile
This season marks the seventh year
Seven...
May you rest in peace in heaven
We miss you, Andy

The Big Sixty

As he opens up the month of June...
Oh my dayzzzz
If you were here
What an excitement we would share
Bank Holiday vibes
Would've been real nice
With Champagne flowing
Glasses clinking
Music blaring
And all of us mesmerised by what you are wearing
Smiles and laughter as we cheer
And celebrate your **60th** year
Oh what joy we would all share.

Today, bro,
I shall try my hardest not to shed a tear
I know you'll be celebrating up there
Dancing with the angels
With a band of heavenly music
(I'm sure the steel pan is somewhere)
But how I wish you were right here
So I could hug you saying Happy Birthday
And you grin and reply, 'Yeah Yeah'
Oh boy, here I go

Sitting on the tube and my eyes sting and feel wet
The day hasn't gone into full swing yet
And here I am, just missing you more today
I just wanna SHOUT sometimes and ask
'WHY WAS YOU TAKEN AWAY'
But I'll get that answer one fine day
When I breathe my final breath and eternally with you, I'll stay
Well, bro, there's nothing more I can say but
Happy 60TH Birthday Oh angel of mine
The day will be nice
Sun is already blaring
And my love for you I will never stop sharing.
I will be fine
All my love, brother
Before I cry and someone says, 'What's the matter, my dear?'
I will end and say one last time...
'Cheers' and 'Yeah Yeah'

Setting Aside Time
to Celebrate You

I awoke before the sun
I sang in my heart before the birds
Smelled the flowers in my room
Some still not in full bloom
And I sit on the edge of my bed
Memories of you fill my head
Still images
Moving gestures
Your smile and your laughter
Ha-ha, bro, memory of your dance makes me dizzy
But let me still put on some music
Before the tears crush my spirit
How I miss you
How I miss you so damn much
Oh man, I've done it now... that one thought,
And my cheeks are wet to the touch
Chest feels tight
As the day breaks and puts an end to the night
I welcome the 1st of June
You open the doors of summer.
When you were here,
You'd start your day with champagne to cheer another year

If I didn't have to work today, I'd lift a glass for you this morning
But as soon as my working day ends, it's me and you, bro
Oh dear, the dams have broken!
My heart surrenders to the pain of loss
This year marks ten, since you left us back then
But you never left my spirit and my soul
I close my eyes and there you are
Holding my hands smiling...
Yes, there you are...
I play out the vision, hold out my arms
Reaching out to kiss you, fist bumps and we laugh
The bottle pops, we fill our glasses
Happy Birthday, Bro
It's June at last
The sun is somewhere, for there is morning light
It's hiding like a birthday surprise
I breathe
Or is it a sigh?
Happy Birthday to you Happy Birthday
As I sing to you this Stevie Wonder song
(It is always the best version)
Let me dry my eyes
Dance like Andy danced
And fall in a fit of laughter
No one can seriously dance like you
You took your steps to heaven
So dance today, my brother
I will dance with you in my heart

Ah there it is... the sun has risen
Traffic starts to flow
And the birds are singing
Let me pray.
Time to start the day

Happy Birthday, Alipaly

Oh the joy
I'm like a child that receives a new toy
The one that stays up on Christmas Eve
To peep at her goodies under the tree
It's the gratefulness of living another year
Others whose lives were lost
Loved ones left to be comforted by the cross
I smile
The world's been cruel since last year
But God kept me
And His love for me shines bright
Never have I seen before the colours in rain
Hidden rainbows of God's promises
Washing away grief's pain
May there be not another George Floyd
Let love and unity fill a prejudiced void
Bless the Lord, oh my soul and all that's within me, Yes I
bless Your Holy name
When I think of all the blessings I have obtained
Once again... I thank You for keeping me, guiding me,
teaching me, holding me when my heart's been broken
When words have been left unspoken
Happy Birthday to me, Alipaly
I sang as I entered into my birthday,

I danced with no shame
Happy am I as I proclaim His name
And rejoice all the things He's got me through
Today I share with you
My craziness
My love
My laughter
My joy
Today I celebrate life
Like a child that receives a brand new toy
The one that stays up on Christmas Eve
To peep at her goodies under the tree
My brother opened June's door
At the end of this day, I'll shut its door
And ask God in His mercy, like I did in past years...
'Lord grant me one more'

One Last Entry, One Last Time, One Last Rhyme

My stomach feels empty
My heart beats quietly in my chest
As thoughts and memories surround me
Today seems a little hard to digest
You'd think by now my spirit would be still
That when his anniversary approaches, I'll just get on with
life and chill
Well, it's not so simple.
Don't get me wrong
As time has gone by, I have become strong
But there's that little part of me, I can't deny
That pinches my heart till my soul wants to cry
And I rock thinking of that day
Why did you die?
Who took you away?
I don't blame God, it's Him who has carried me
Lovingly shadowed me
Gave me visions to give me peace and let my emotions
run free
Today I feel empty
Not because I am hungry
It's that pinch that gripes me
Longing to see him dance

Not because he could... more to the fact he can't

Longing to hear him laugh, his voice

To hear him say, 'Yeah Yeah,' and smell his cologne linger in the air

I know this time every year

I feel compelled to share

The love of a brother

Which quite frankly compares to no other

It was Good Friday the sixth of April

That on my knees I crumpled and fell

As I saw him through the cracks of the door

Laying there, very still on the cold wooden floor

Reality hadn't hit that he breathed no more.

I couldn't get up

I used my arms to help me slide towards him

Every ounce of energy left my limbs as I pulled myself closer.

Then I went blind

Not because my physical eyesight left me

But it was the curtain of tears that welled up so I couldn't see

I cried

I cried

I cried

I cried

And I cried

It was the commotion of family in and outside that woke me to the fact Chris really died

And I cried

And I wailed
Held my breath, for the cry stuck and found it hard to exhale.
No... The memory has not gone
Yet I have over the years learnt to move and carry on
It's just this weekend for some reason my spirit was uneven
I kept busy
Tidied up and cooked till there was nothing left to season
Had my sister round so there was a good reason
We laughed, we drank, we ate till very late
Next day spent with Sis E and Sis Honey
So, to be honest I'm ok
Just have these li'l moments, but hey
And now as I've let out this wave of emotions on paper...
I'm ready to start my day
The sun is shining through my curtains
And its warmth feels like a kiss from the heavens
It's the sixth
And...
Come on, Alipaly, get up, put some music on,
Let me dance while I make up my bed
Shaking the sadness trying to build up in my head
Remembering Andy alive and not dead
His smile
His charm
His laughter
His love
But most of all his dance to the rhythm of the lyrics

I thank my God upon every remembrance of you

—Philippians 1:3

7
FRIENDSHIP AND FAMILY

Best Friends and Family Love

Nothing beats family love, although real good friends come close, and best friends closer still.

It is true, as they say, 'You can't choose your family, but you can choose your friends.' As they come, stay and leave in different stages of our lives, it is best to listen to our mothers' advice at a very early age! I'm sure yours said just like mines, 'Show me your friends, and I'll show you you.' I can gladly and proudly say I chose well. I've never had just one best friend at any one time. As a group, I had firm favourites as a child, although my innermost secrets of abuse I never shared in those tender years. They were just great friends to hang around with and have fun. To be honest, in my childhood, my bestie was my god sister Marion. We did everything together during our school holidays.

It wasn't until my late teens that I struck up a really close friendship with three girls who grew into beautiful women, such valuable women who are godparents to my children, and we remain such wonderful friends to this very day. Kudos to Bernie, Tracey and Kim, truly sincere friends who I hold highly in my life although we don't see each other hardly at all now. Kim lives abroad, and Bernie,

Tracey and I are so busy in our own lives and live quite a distance apart. Bernie is still my 'go to girl' when I need to offload life and share ideas. She holds within her great wisdom, and her advice is loving, caring but firm.

As an adult, married twice with children, I've developed long, meaningful friendships, not just with women but men, too. They have become my big brothers to add to the blood ones I already had. These friendships were so different from the ones in my teens to a certain extent, as most of my friendships in my later years were with married couples with children, and we had a different kind of connection. Especially when I became a born-again Christian in my thirties.

My blood sisters are also my best friends, especially Ann. The other two live in America, so we love each other from afar, but boy, do I love them. Ann is a gem, always there for me. She listens and she talks. She tells me off, but we also have the greatest belly laughs. She is my favourite travel companion to Trinidad, and Mum would say my bad influencer due to daily rum-drinking, morning till night. No no no, not drunkards (lol) but to have a good lime (the Trini word for hanging out with friends is 'we liming') with holiday vibes (terrible, I know; naughty me—slap my hand!) Yeah, me and my sis.

Then there's my bonified sis; I call her my twin. We laugh and think alike, and she knows EVERYTHING about me… well, 90%. Do we really know every striking thing about a person? Some things are best left dead unsaid! Lord, take me before You take her!!

Vee—this woman; if best friends are the ones you go everywhere with, laugh till you pee yourself (which isn't hard at our age), cry together, support each other, then drive you mad with their foolishness and have smoke coming out your ears, then yes, she fits into that bracket nicely.

Finally, my family. Lord, I love this mad lot to bits, and I pray they come to know God as I have.

I Thank God for Friends
Like You

In the world I've had quite a few
But the secrets of my heart they never knew
Whenever my heart felt frail
They'd cheer me up and treat me to paint my nails
'Put on your dancing shoes and let's have a ball
Have a rum
Have a lager
Come on, girl, cheer up and have another
'Flutter your eyes at that guy over there
If the man at home is stressing you out
Swap him, that will shut his mouth'

But was that what I wanted to hear?
Their words were loose, but I know they cared
I called them friends true and dear
Although they didn't always know the best for my welfare
I didn't always take their advice
Although I came close more than thrice
I thought alcohol was the only way to feel nice

One day an old friend witnessed to me about a love
everlasting
It was from a man who died and paid a high price

His name, none other than Jesus Christ
What a day when I met salvation
When I realised the truth about our creation

I stepped into a church called The Potter's House
Looking back at my life's walk
Learnt it was my old friend who was born-again
Spent years praying for me
I met his beautiful wife
And she became my friend, worth more than ten

She's rebuked me in the gentle way
Even helped me learn how to pray
She is there for me night and day
Never finds me a bother, never turns me away
The fellowships
The nice long chats
Been there, done that, so she knew first hand where I was at
Tenderly showing me the right words to say
Showing me lovingly what dress is okay
Helping me to understand God's word
And if she's not entirely sure,
She'll lead me to knock on pastor's door
When my heart is feeling frail
She'll find a scripture to heal the crack
And set me right back on track

Don't read me wrong, she is not the only one
Many a true friend have I found in The Potter's House crew

I've learnt a lot from friends like you
I hope I can befriend a new convert and also see them
through
I'm so glad Christ is in my life
And I pray that my friends from yesteryear
May one day see the light
Abandon their foolish ways
The raves
The smoking and drinking
The hangover days

They think I have changed
Seem very strange
That is all right by me
As I have an awesome testimony
God took this bit of broken clay
And melted all the sin away
Blood washed He remoulded me
Baptised by Holy Ghost fire, I proclaim I'm set free

So big up all my church crew, old, young and new
Singles, couples and the pastors and their wives
God sees and His reward is in lieu
Which leads me to say in love again
'I thank God for friends like you.'

A Prayer for the Family

Birds of a feather flock together
Or so the saying goes
I wonder if the same could be said
For families with the same godhead

Although the same God they praise
Each Sunday they go their separate ways
Church for one down south
One gone up north
The rest on the east-west corridor

Why don't they come together as one anymore?
Maybe too many words spoken that crippled the heart
Living in the one house but miles apart
When did this start?
When will it finish?
The modern-day family is in crisis

No longer are they praying together
The attitude now is 'whenever—whatever'
As for mines, there is a burning passion within me
I yearn for the salvation of my extended family
Why won't they listen though?
Why won't they comprehend?

Jesus is coming back!

They have to straighten up their act
Know which friends to keep and those to back-back
Then there's the music, lustful lyrics...
Just listen carefully to what you hear
Make sure it's worthy for your ears
I won't speak any more on it
Lest tempers flare

Give me the strength, Lord
The will to keep on
Wisdom in speech and guard my tongue
Let my life be a testimony
To touch each one
From the eldest of my family
To the youngest one

Help me not to live in fear
Let us come together in prayer
Unify us keep our love strong
Unveil the living word
Let them see and learn the truth
That Jesus is the living son
Who bared excessive wounds on Calvary
Now we can inherit salvation
And be free of the weight of the enemy

Paint the blood of the lamb over my family's name
Let not any marriage vows in our generations become a lie
Help them fulfil their duties of mother, father, children,
husband and wife
May my past be a lesson to teach
And Christian marriage counsellors be at an easy reach

Surely my family will make it
Every lie from the enemy shattered
Every demon that shook us scattered
Honour and glory to You, Our King
Who washed us clean
I pray you cast any sinful ways
In the sea of forgetfulness
I pray for there to be spiritual growth
And one day all my family
Would be seated at the foot of Your throne
AMEN.

My Sister, My Angel, Sandra E

I never knew angels walked on their feet
Or belched from their heart after they eat
Or laughed heheheee when something sweet dem sweet

I tell yuh it's true
She can even cook a wicked rice 'n' peas and curry mutton
stew
And if you need a prayer partner
Just call on this here prayer warrior

She is no normal angel you see
God listens to her as she pours out her heart
She asks and He hears
He responds, she prepares
Guarantee when awesome things happen to me
I know it is because that angel of mine was interceding to JC

With this angel none can compare
Come rain or shine she is always there
She's not what you call a fairweather friend
She will stick like glue to you until the bitter or sweet end

Sometimes, when we get saved and come to Christ
Our families get worried and cause all sorts of strife

Suddenly from a family of five
You stand alone
Unsteady on your feet as you face the unknown

Well, I'm leaving to start a new life in a foreign land
I shan't be selfish; I'll lend you a hand
I cannot take my awesome angel with me
As she has a husband and four children you see
Even her own business taking care of God's lost children
Making sure they get a glimpse of their Father of Creation
I simply can't take her away from all these God given ministries
Now, if you are trustworthy and won't let me down
I'll lend you my angel until I return
And in her presence many qualities you will learn.

Sisters... A Time of Dedication

There comes a time
When things are not quite fine
And you call out
'God, give me a sign'

There comes a time
When you're filled with jubilation,
And there's that special someone
You call on to share without hesitation

There comes a time
When the cares of your world
Are too much to behold
But there's always that someone you can rely on

There comes a time
For decisions to be made
And you call on Christ
Plus, that friendship that He gave

There comes a time
When you sit back and reflect
The joys
The pain

The shame
The happiness of much
The kind encouraging words
And giving of time
A hand to hold with a gentle touch
A jewel
A precious stone
A friendship that fills my heart
A sisterhood that's set apart

True friendship is often rare
And there are certain times you must declare and show
appreciation
Like birthdays to celebrate
Mother's Days,
You know, just random special days
To give them undivided attention
So, without further ado
I would like to say to all of you
Yes, you know who you are
From my birth you helped name me
From teenage and college years we had no fear
From salvation to now we have grown
May God grant my besties
The desires of their hearts

There comes a time
And the time has come

To dedicate to you
This poem to show my love come what may
And I am blessed having you all in my life

Big Sis

She's a joy
She's a queen in her own right
A beauty in everyone's sight
She's so talented
Such a delight
Makes designer clothes
With her eyes closed tight!
Always there for me
Through stormy seas and calm rivers
I am blessed to have you, Ann, as my big sis
And truly appreciate your love and kindness
Gosh when you turned SIXTY!! What the heck
I had to count back and double check...
As that number didn't seem right
What a wonderful testimony of life
Still more adventures to be had
And with you by my side, would make me glad
I send you a blessing
Of love and fullness of joy
For increased prosperity
And that your cup will never run empty

My sister, Ann
Such a blessing you are

Shines like the bright morning star
No matter near or far
You are just there
We talk and laugh on the phone
Enjoy holidays on our own
And let's not forget the outfits you've sown
My goodness
I love the fact you design your own.
Clever
Classy
Sassy
Always got my back
When I'm with you smiles never lack
I'm blessed
When we're together
Barman don't need to ask us twice
It's a vodka & tonic
Straight rum on ice
Cheers, big sis, and everything niiiiice
I smile as I think of my fifty-odd years
You've been there to share my laughter and tears
I'm thankful
Not only are you beautiful
But you have wisdom beyond your years
With you beside me
There's nothing in life I'll fear.

Family, where, according to my niece, Shivs,
Is where love begins and never ends.

When I Look At Vee I See…

A woman who has run out of breath
She has dropped to the deepest depths
And struggles to place her feet to climb back up each step.

A hidden smile encaged in the outward smile on her face
That if you look closely resembles a mosaic tile
Pieces of life that have stuck together
And weather life's storms and that's where the lies form…

'Yes, I'm ok. Yes, I'm having a wonderful day.
Yes, my children respect what I say, Yes, I'm in control…
Yes, Yes, YES… I am whole.'

I look at Vee and she sheepishly looks away from me
A half-risen eye, she sags her shoulders and sighs…
'What's the point of living? I just want to give up and die.'

I have no answers for her pain is rare,
I dwell on my hurts,
I rummage in my mind, searching for something to compare…
But I am aware that her past holds much despair
And her future, alas, is filled with fear.

Shall it always be so?
Will her spirit and soul stay crushed down so low?
No, I tell you, not while I'm here
Jesus left and the Helper came
And assuredly, I say to you, 'In His book I see your name.'

Not condemned by shame,
Not a bruised lamb injured and lame,
But a victorious winner who beat the devil at his own game.

Oh how my eyes behold such a vision...
The beauty, the grace...
'Is this a mirage, an illusion?? Surely this is not the same woman?!'
A figment of my imagination?

Ha-ha no, no, no
It is the woman who for years bowed her head low,
With the help of Jesus
Her walk of salvation she gallantly shows

The mask is off,
I see a reflection of me, but God's redeeming love has set us both free
I see Veronica as never before,
This woman is armed and ready for war
Who will come first to be kicked and beaten to the floor?
You abuse,
You drought,

You spirit of ugliness that tries to hush her mouth???
Come, let me call you out like legion
And go tell your master Vee has stepped into her season

A season of wealth
A season of joy and to claim
Everything the enemy stole in your name

Lift your head and shake off the dust
This is the word from the Lord so you simply must
Great is His name and with His loving arms around you,
you live in a stronger frame
His care embraces you and He whispers in your ear
'You can do it, you can do it, trust in Me, I'm right here

Sandra & Ali, I sent to be your friends for life
Trouble will come, trouble will go
They may not have all the answers but strong support
they'll show.

What do I see when I look at Vee?

A woman who's learnt to smile and laugh,
A woman whose beauty God took His time to graft
A mirror of His image, that's why she glows
I see love
I see strength that has risen from the deepest depths where
she wept
Now hope floats, strength and boldness have arisen,

A skilled writer and a poem maker...
At times I can't lie,
I just want to shake her!

Opportunities of great things are embedded within,
God's angels start to unravel, and I hear multiple chains drop
The devil's plans have been uncovered
And his plans for destruction have flopped

I see love
I see her smile,
We sit and talk for a while
Gently poking each other after completing another mile.
Laughter fills the air
We sure do make a great pair
Hurts and pains together we'll share
With Sandra, we are intricately entwined
Our fragile stance is now lined with the presence of God

I will now declare and decree
Great is the woman I see in Vee.

My Brothers & Me

My goodness gracious me
What can I say about my big brothers
Anthony & Learie?
My biggest loves
Along with my sons, grandson and God above

I couldn't want more in my life
Than these two bros
So helpful, protective, loving and kind
So many memories come to mind

Like Lee, when we were children
He constantly teased me.
Scaring and chasing after me
With dead flies on pins, bumblebees
Spiders and creepy crawlies in his hands
Not forgetting the worms on sticks
But I got my own back
For when I told Mum or Dad, he was sure to get licks

Anthony to some was called Tony
But we at home nicknamed him Bones
And so, it's stuck all these years
The reason why, people have never known

I'm sure it was Lee who gave him that name
To call him anything different now wouldn't be the same.

Bones was and still is my protector
Never stands back to be a spectator
He intervenes when he sees things going wrong
Always got my back
I know he's got me
No time is ever too long
Picks me up when my health is down
Gives me lectures saying, 'Sis, you must rest
It will get you better faster, it's for the best'
So, I listen, sometimes with a frown
But I know he is right
Yet I get busy when he is out of sight
But you know that saying
'Those who don't hear will feel and learn!'
As he is bigger than me
I surrender,
I know he's behind my healing testimony

Learie, he is a joker
Every time we meet, we're in fits of laughter
He also takes time out when he's out and about
To give his little sis a shout
Both my brothers are great dancers
When the music plays
You'd best get out the way
Always the highlight of the night

Seeing them on the dance floor
Their moves you've never seen before
I try to follow, but don't always get my feet quite right

Skilled carpenters, interior decorators
Creative minds
New bespoke designs just for you
Houses, beach huts and offices
Become brand new
Ryan Interiors... that's Lee's business name
Look on Insta
I bet you'll want to book.

Well, you know by now I lost one
And life has never been the same
We held each other in our worst bout of sadness
Encouraging words
Accompanied with the greatest of hugs
Long conversations of our dreams and aspirations

We've seen each other at our lowest
Saying one to another
Never give up
Always aspire to aim higher
But these two brothers of mine
Just makes my whole world shine
Pray for them daily in Jesus' name
Bones is already in the race, fighting a good fight
Lord, help Learie see God's light

Hear His voice and make that choice
That choice…

To surrender all
And allow God to lead him to his destiny
Creating powerful testimonies
Great are my brothers, Bones and Lee
Love them to infinity
I feel so safe when they are around
So proud of the men they are
They beat many by far

Yes, love you both unconditionally
Thank you from my heart for always looking out for me
May God continually bless the two of you.

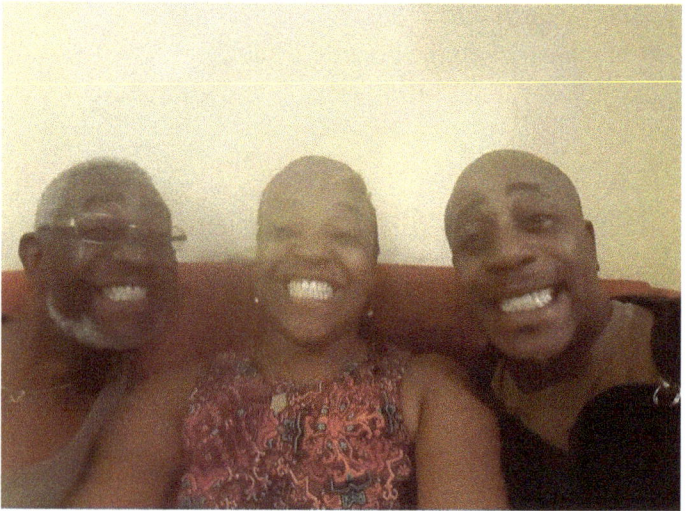

As iron sharpens iron,
So a man sharpens the countenance of his friend.

—Proverbs 27:17

And let us consider one another in order to stir up love
and good works.

—Hebrews 10:24

Greater love has no one than this, than to lay down
one's life for his friends.

—John 15:13

8
REFLECTION

Let's Focus on You

Life sure does have its rollercoasters, be it school life, dealing with bullies or young gangs trying to reel you in to do the same foolishness as them, teenage girls de-valuing their self-worth by dressing provocatively, having boyfriends too young, or teenage boys trying too hard to act like men.

Are you fed up? Has going out every Friday and Saturday night lost its pull on you? Are you tired of faking it, chatting, laughing, drinking and smoking. Then, when you get home, you literally slump to the floor, wondering what's it all for?
Who, really, are you trying to impress?

Do you feel lost and alone as a single mum? Did you have kids too young before your own life begun? Now look: evenings stuck looking at homework books, preparing dinner, putting kids in the shower, washing clothes, and when you think you've finished, you spot another load. And each day repeats itself in a cycle. Yes, you love your children, but surely there is more. Something is missing. You feel dull, half-empty rather than half-full!

You want a better future. You want to turn your life around, but you feel burnt out and just can't get off the ground.

Men, I see you;some of you reek of problems. Find it hard to transition from boys to men. You want to change your ways, stop being abusive and angry, lazy-minded and be free from drug and alcohol abuse and lust.

But how? Who can help? Who can redeem you, fix all your mistakes and lead you in a direction that will change your life forever?

I can tell you. I know of a man who laid down His life for His friends. He was falsely accused, battered and bruised, spat on, hands and feet hammered to wood with nails, wearing a crown of thorns that pierced his head. He carried the weight of every sin imaginable. His name: none other than Jesus Christ,

The good news is that He is no longer dead. He rose three days after He was sacrificed and is very much alive. He did it all for me and you to cast away every bondage of sin and make the way for us to all have access to God once again. When we become born-again of the Spirit, we, too, have the right to live for all eternity in Heaven with God. Yes, we are His friends and joint heirs with Jesus Christ.

Jesus made the way for you, my brothers and sisters. Every worry, every sin, every difficult situation you find yourself in, just come to Him, and I promise you, He can and will set you free. All you must do is pray, trust and believe.

I pray this section speaks to you and stirs your Spirit to reach out and touch the hem of His garment. He knocks and waits for you to let Him in.

Our Brother's Hand

Who are we but mere sinners that fall time and time again
Who is God, that in these times,
Stretches out His hands,
And we stretch out our own to brace ourselves to get back
up again

Leaning on His word and awesome plan for our lives
Do not suffer yourselves, my sisters my brothers
With the sometimes deafening lies from satan and his
helpers
The voices of despair, failure and fear
Of rejection, blame and unjustified shame

Is not the God we serve one, yet still the Trinity...
Father, Spirit and Son?
The promises laid out for each one of us are like twins –
Different but the same
So do not wear yourselves thin, recaptured by sin

Lift your voices and proclaim the authority in His name
By the density of His pain
The devil was slain
And our lives once again
Has a link to Our Father

Now we may outstretch our hands and hold tight to Jesus
Who is Himself our brace and who covers us with God's
grace

Yes, we are sinners that fall from time to time
But in Jesus, we always have a lifeline.

'Call to Me, and I will answer you, and show you great and mighty things, which you do not know.'

—Jeremiah 33:3 NKJV

Talk to Me

Pray pray, I say
Pray in the evening
Pray without ceasing
Pray with conviction
Pray in exaltation
Pray in the morning
Just before the birds sings and bring the dawn in
Don't be like the disciples and kneel yawning

Pray pray, I say
Pray for a new day
Pray to walk in His way

Pray in your heart He'll always stay
Pray that He strips you and has His way
Pray for your daughters pray for your sons
Pray for the life in the womb that's already begun

Pray for strength
Pray for diligence
Pray for the Almighty to send deliverance

Pray for salvation
For the earth's population

Pray eyes be open and God's word freely spoken

Pray for the broken
Pray to be shaken
Eyes sharp as a falcon
Wings of an eagle
Flying high to every corner of the earth and sky

Pray for revival
Pray for a new birth

Pray pray, I say
God is eager to have His day
Wars and rumours of wars
Politicians and leaders prostituting the land
Earthquakes and hurricanes like never before
Touching the most unlikely of shores

Are you not worried, have you not stopped to think??
Your life could be over after the next blink
Your life could be over sooner than you think
Pray... Pray... just Pray
God is ready, desperate, waiting, yearning, listening... Even
if it's just a whisper... kneel and give your life to Jesus today.
Come Pray.

Arise

The light goes out
Sit still...ssshhhhh
There—do you hear that voice?
'Arise,' He says, 'take action'

Don't let your dreams drift away like soft cotton clouds in
the sky

It's time to stand
Let those dreams burst forth with that inner passion that
surges with force

People, get ready to turn your lights back on
Refocus, get back…
Yes, rebirth your vision
The Holy Spirit will be a surgeon to make that incision
Reach in
Take action to ease it out
Do you feel it...
That Greatness??...

It's In You
God's power ignites with prayer
This new week, a new month draws near

The words in my heart to you I share
My heart's a little heavy
With memories of Good Friday's nightmare
Many years ago
But the Holy Spirit brings peace, love and joy
It blankets death and brings forth life
Those who know will understand as I gently hold his spiritual hand
(Miss you, my brother)

I smile as I walk in the fruits of the Spirit
Commanding the morning for the goodness we shall inherit.

Stand with your armour on
Lift your voices in a praise and worship song
For your breakthrough won't be long
With Christ leading
And the Holy Spirit inside of you
You shall stand strong.

²² But the fruit of the Spirit is love, joy, peace, longsuffering, kindness, goodness, faithfulness,²³ gentleness, self-control. Against such there is no law.

—Galatians 5:22-23

The Calling

Wake up, dude
Smell the good food
Don't you understand?
God has a plan
So, what's the scam, my man?

I know God spoke you a word
Don't be playing like you never heard
No, no don't be playing like you get jittery nerves
Can't you see, there is purpose for you and me?
God shall use us to suit our credibility
You prayed for strengthening and direction
God stood back and had you under inspection

If the Alpha and Omega, the great I Am
Knows you fit the description
Who are you to run and hide,
Stick your head in the sand
And turn a blind eye?
You tremble now because you know God heard your cry
You are thinking now, 'Can I, can I?'
Well God says, 'Yes, you can,'
So, stand up, my man

Stand solid and strong
Stand on the foundation
That God helped you build on
If God took time out to speak to you a word
Can you not see, my brother?
This is not damnation
Give Him some help here
A little co-operation

It is a love so strong
That will help you along
It is a love so rare
None on earth can compare
It is the love of a skilled Sculptor
At work with his clay
He will break you
Mould you
Fill you
And guide you

So, wake up, dude
There is work to be done
Do not be frightened
God has called you, my son

Fireproof

Picture this…
Have you ever put something on the stove?
When it's finished you take it off
Only in the process, you burnt yourself
You had no cloth, you were careless
Remember how the intense heat of the burn made you jump?
Your hands pull back in a quick reflex
You rush to run it under cold water
But too late
It's gone deep, turned red then black
See where I'm getting at?

A plain fact
You cannot handle the heat on a patch of skin
But if you carry on blind to your sin, hell's fire is where you'll fall in
No cold water
No soothing ointments
No reflex action to jump from the heat
Nowhere to run
No temperature control
No waiting for winter to come
Or raining season to begin
No autumn breeze to cool the pain

No energy to live
No way to die
Can't see where the screams are coming from
Why? Because hell has burnt your eyes.
Is living your sin worth this predicament to be in?

There is a battle going on between the mind and heart
A tug of war between the body and soul
Sensible thinking wants to lead you home
Conviction in attack, you want to turn back
You've read the Bible
You know the truth, the facts
But sinful thoughts are tugging at you
Yet you pretend that part of the word you never knew

New York, Washington—the world under demolition

Global disunity, a call for a One-World Religion
It's in the news
Or have you not stopped to listen

To fall in love with an unsaved person would destroy your
soul
Telling you words that make you want to go astray
But to walk away from Jesus
With your life, you will pay
To the backslider, I say slide back
End this devil's ruthless attack
Shake him off from riding your back

Spiritual love is what you need
Not the worldly love
In that, you will never succeed

Do not worry, Jesus will not leave you alone
He is the Husband to the widower and Father to the
fatherless
He will lead you to His throne
What is the matter?

Have you fallen too deep
In the night, can you not sleep?
On your pillow are stains of tears
Because you know your life is wrong
And you are full of fear
Why live in such despair?
Turn to Christ and He'll start the repair

So, tell me... Are you dipping yourself in worldly attire?
It is not what your heart desires
But it is what the devil requires
he will lead you in the wrong direction
By filling your head with all kinds of deception
But can you afford to listen to his lies?
For in the end, you will surely die.
Peak your ears to God's distinctive voice
He will lead you to the altar
There, you must make a choice.
Choose wisely

Remember the promises you have read
Let Him lead you from the living dead
And breathe new life in you
Sweet union with the Godhead

Jesus will clothe you in His Majesty
To listen and read His word
'Come.' Jesus says, 'follow Me'
And He'll lead you into an eternity of tranquillity

Liar!

You thought you got me
Had me pinned down by lead
You gave me an illness
That messed up my head
You planned for me to stay that way till ah dead
Ha! That illness is blood washed now
Salvation brought me to a place
Where I can have pleasure to stamp on your face
And tell you plainly, stay in your own fire

Devil man, you are just a liar

To think you robbed me of my speech
Gave me vertigo
So I could not walk down my street
Tried to keep me locked up inside
So I couldn't hear a saved man street preach
You actually thought you could keep me from God
Get it into your thick head

That the Trinity can see right through you
You are really a weak little speck in that great huge fire

Devil man, you are just a liar

Since I came to Christ, you really trippin'
The fact I'm where I belong
Is really rattling your cage
You try to trip me up
Still trying to attack me
You are so bitter
So full of rage
Every bad thing you throw at me
God changes for good
Every trial and oppression
God pulls me through with faith stronger than ever
So, whatever!

Don't you understand, little devil man
Salvation has brought all us Christians to a place
Where we can take great pleasure to stamp on your face
You are under our feet
We will stamp so hard
You won't be able to creep
And the joy of it is more souls are being saved everyday
All the gunge you covered them with
Has been washed away

HA! In yuh face
We are free by God's grace
devil just retire in your own fire
So insignificant compared to The Messiah

devil man, you are a great fat liar

As Time Passes

Are you ready?
Tick... Tock... Tick... Tock...
Are your hands raised in praise?
Are you ready for the second phase?
Tick... Tock... Tick...
Have you turned from your sinful ways?
Are you ready?
Tock... Tick... Tock...
Your life is running against the clock
Time is running and passing
The hour is drawing near
Is it today, tomorrow or next year?
He said He is coming back

His word is valid, strong, it has no slack
Look at the news, sit back and sigh
What is this world coming to?
Read it!
The Bible has the answers
All truth and no lies
It will stare you dead in your face—
Signs of the times, it's taking place

Wars in the Holy Land
Earthquakes in England
Cyclones like never before
Natural disasters that happen unnaturally

The dysfunctional misgivings of the modern-day family
Children bearing children
Parents wanting to be their children's best friend
Fathers and husbands forget how to be men
They are even crying out for one ruler to bring peace
So all the fighting and wars may cease

Huh... I tell you,
Go on in your ways,
Keep on listening to what those scientists say
Global warming, ozone layer deforming
Listen, my friend
God wants all men
To bow down and accept Him as their own
That we may together praise Him at the foot of His throne
To be happy through all eternity
Get down on your bended knee
Give your life to The Trinity

Are you ready?
Tick... Tock... Tick... Tock
Are you ready?
Do you think, I mean, really think you can handle seven
years' tribulation?

What makes you think you are strong enough for that situation?

Tick... Tock
And in the blink of an eye
Time stops.

that if you confess with your mouth the Lord Jesus and believe in your heart that God has raised Him from the dead, you will be saved.

—Romans 10:9

For with the heart one believes unto righteousness, and with the mouth confession is made unto salvation.

—Romans 10:10

Nor is there salvation in any other, for there is no other name under heaven given among men by which we must be saved.

—Acts 4:12

For God so loved the world that He gave His only begotten Son, that whoever believes in Him should not perish but have everlasting life.

—John 3:16

The Big Bang Theory

I boarded a plane in Toronto
Onward to Seattle I was to go
The plane took off into a southern breeze
And I sat back in my chair with ease
The pilot dipped the aircraft side to side
To give his passengers a little tour guide

As the sights of the American plains hit me
I gasped in amazement at God's creativity
Looking in awe as the Holy Spirit filled me
And I realised that there are parts of this world that my
eyes will never see
Which God in His magnificence brought forth to existence

My eyes gazed out over Minneapolis
Full of canyons and caves
Lakes with rippling waves
Each mountain,
Each rock
My eyes glazed with tears as I tried to take stock

From the sky, you can see how the mountains take shape
Only God could have been the Artist to make them take form
They fell in synchronised patterns with valleys in-between

On one side are fields of fir trees
In stunning bright green
Streams running over
And in-between the sandy rocks
Only great love could have designed how they entwined

A BIG BANG! Are they crazy?
Surely out of their mind
An explosion leaves destruction, death and distress
Rubble and dusty cloud storms
Which choke you to death
Where blood runneth over
Screams from every mouth
Mourning and grieving
Blackness over the aftermath

How silent is a whisper in your ear?
A sweet and tender love song
That makes you cry when you hear
Words that speak the truth
Words you can trust
Words that make you feel love without the lust
With every breath exhaled came the words of existence, in order and precision
Without any mistakes or collision
God said, 'Let there be.' and there was
'Become.' and it became, because
He is an awesome God of great signs and wonders
He is a Potter, a Sculptor, the Hallowed Jehovah

To think satan tries to this day to steal the land
Making it ugly and crooked
Wasted desert lands

Take heed
Take note
I make no joke
The day of our Lord is at hand
Repent quickly of your sins
Know where to stand
God has the strength and ability
To reclaim His land
No no, don't shake your head and turn the page
I saw with my own eye's unspoilt artistry
My God is I AM, there is no compromise

Do you really want to go into a lake of fire for eternity and
burn?
Is that what you yearn?
To scream,
No arms to reach out into the darkness
Fire and torture forever
No-one to hear you shout...
Well, I'm telling you,
That's what hell's about

When next you take an airline jet
Look out the window
You might not see what you expect

Forget the buildings (those man-made chores)
But look to the hills, valleys, lakes and mountains
The forests, canyon, ocean and sea
No-one but God could have brought them forth with His
own breath
A world with Him should be all you require
Not the alternative
That is to dwell in hell's fire

Today is the day of your salvation, saith God.
That is My desire.

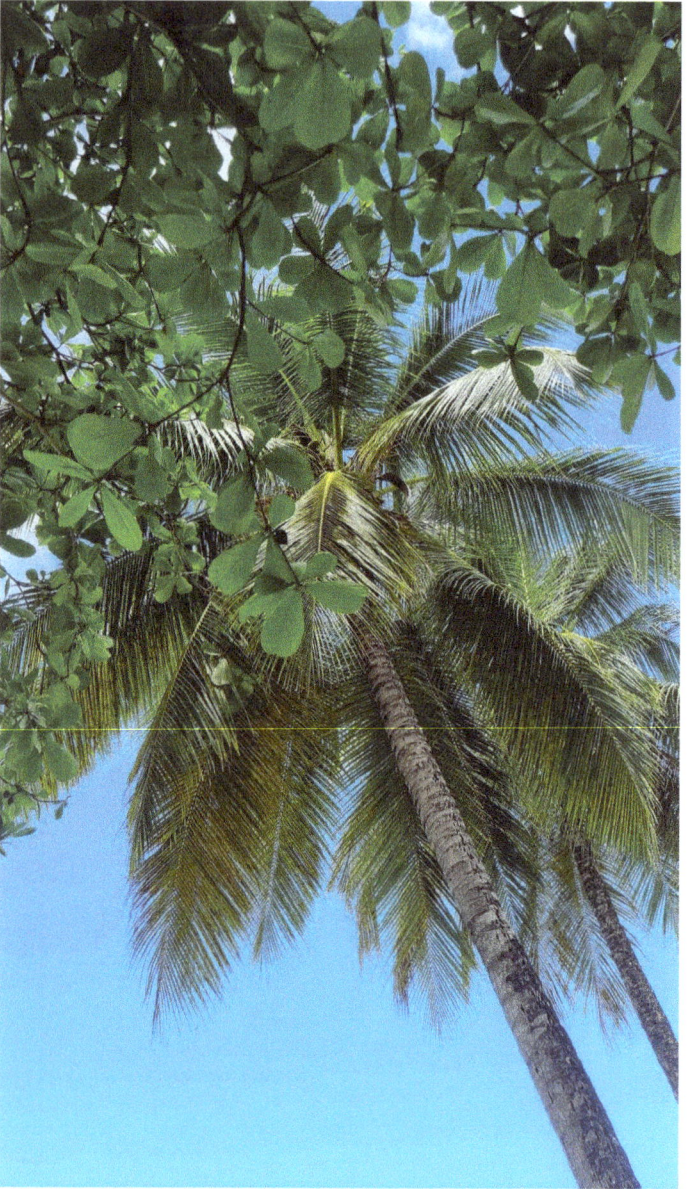

Greatness

The light goes out
Sit still... ssshhhh
There—do you hear that voice?
'Arise,' He says, 'take action, it's time to take your life back'

Don't let your dreams drift away like soft cotton clouds in
the sky

It's time to stand
Let those dreams burst forth with that inner passion that
surges with force

People, get ready to turn your lights back on
Refocus, get back
Yes, rebirth your vision
Jesus will be a surgeon to make that incision
Reach in
Take action to ease it out
Do you feel it...
That Greatness??...

It's In You
God's power ignites with prayer
As the weeks, months and years draw near

The words in my heart with you I share
My heart tingles
God will lead you in His care
And as a witness, I too shall declare
Telling of your testimony that led you there
Don't be afraid
Take that step
God's promises to you He's always kept
So, on your marks...
Get set...
Go

Jesus answered and said to him, 'Most assuredly, I say to you, unless one is born again, he cannot see the kingdom of God.' —John 3:3

Sinners Prayer
(Prayer for Salvation)

To free yourself from the bondage of sin
And become born-again into the kingdom of God
Repeat these words with a sincere heart

Lord, I come to you on bended knees
To ask if you can set me, a sinner, free?
I've been told You really love and care for me
And my eyes are now open, I can see.
So right now, I do repent
And turn away from a life ill-spent
I offer up myself to You
I believe You, Jesus, are God's Son
I believe in The Trinity, that You're all three in one
I believe You died on the cross to save the lost
Three days later You arose and defeated death
And now we have a bridge to get to God.
I'm so glad I found You, no longer bound
Come live inside me from now on
I shall raise my hands in worship as I sing You a song
I know now it's with You Jesus, that I belong
And I shall tell of Your goodness all the day long.

Amen

9
TRIBUTES

Tributes

First of all, if you said the Sinner's Prayer like I did back in 1999, I would like to say congratulations and welcome to the family of Christ.

I encourage you to find a church that believes in the baptising of the Holy Spirit with evidence of speaking in tongues, a church that believes and practices the New Testament in its entirety.

They also believe the Bible was written by men divinely inspired by God, and the only way to God is through His son, Jesus Christ.

For an introduction to your Christian walk, start by reading the gospels, the beginning of the New Testament (Matthew, Mark, Luke and John). Start with John to gain a deeper understanding about your salvation.

Tributes—it's always nice to pay homage to someone you value and who has had an impact in your life. It's unfortunate, however, that most times, these tributes and accolades are given when someone has died.

They are not only given at funerals, of course, but they could also show love and appreciation to people who have special birthdays or at celebrations.

I have a few tributes I'd like to share with you: a dear uncle who passed away a few years back and my beautiful auntie who fell victim to that wretched Coronavirus.

One of my best friend's, Vee's, very young great nephew died suddenly, and his mother was desperately distraught and inconsolable. Poems were written for all, and Vee's niece and my aunt's and uncle's families were comforted a small touch by just a few words on a page. I also have a celebration for Vee's granddaughter's special birthday.

There are a few little extras I hope you enjoy.

Darling Auntie Shirley

What it is to breathe your last?
Unimaginable to know
When that time comes to let go
And the glory of God's face begins to show
As you step into His presence face-to-face
Whether or not prematurely, who's to say?
God has ultimate control and His way

It's the stillness
When you hear the news
That a loved one has passed
You scrabble in your mind the last time you spoke
And sigh with a cracked smile as you hear their voices in
your mind
Remembering how sweet and how kind.

Sitting watching the cars go by
Suddenly not even their engines I hear
A numbness has filled the air
The trees sway in a dance of silent breeze
A tear

Hold back the glistening of the eyes
Calm the racing of the heart

Realise the peace my loved one's in
She slipped away
But with that all the pain and artificial breathing ceased
And into the entrance of God's pearly gate
Where a choir of angels await
In harmonious song proclaim she's set free
Of the wretched beast of C19 that invaded her chest...
Now and for all eternity, auntie will have sweet rest
Seated at His feet and on His lap place her head to calmly
sleep

My heart cries
But the same time at peace
She loved the Lord
She's ran her race
Today she gets to kiss His Face
God, Our Father, so full of grace

Today...
So much going on
Places to go, dinner to cook, house to clean
What do I do, what can I say, how do I feel?

Just kneel, just pray

Allow God to steer the day, bring peace
Rejoice, for either way...

He is celebrated
My aunt is transformed
Rest in peace, auntie, my all-time back in the day beautiful
movie star.

Shine Bright

Sweet Sixteen

I stood by your mother's side minute after minute
Encouraging her and saying it wouldn't be long
Down the birth canal you pushed with determination
At the foot of the bed, I guided your head
And then you were here,
Literally without motivation
The most beautiful, most precious baby girl
The memory of your mother's birthing pain
All of a sudden was just that... A memory

I wiped you down
Took your weight
And from my arms to your mother's, I didn't hesitate
We watched you with eyes welled up in tears
Smiled so bright knowing you were now here.

Now look, sixteen already
My oh my, these years have flown by
And I stand in awe as I reflect on your life

You were never a child that brought strife
But joy and smiles, good school reports
Telling silly jokes of all sorts

Everyone always talks of the wonder of your hair
Black, long and beautiful, a quality so rare
But for you, it's part of your natural beauty
You've grown up so much in sixteen years
My heart gets full
And my eyes fill with tears
As I think of that day,
Not so long ago,
That you came into our lives
I held you and didn't want to let go

You'll always be very special to me
My very first granddaughter
God gave you the breath of life
And I had the privilege to deliver you.
My gift of being a midwife to see the task through
I long to see God's plans for you

I know without a shadow of a doubt
He walks side by side with you.
Continue to be the best you can be
Always remembering how special you are to me

Dearest Uncle Wendell

The seed is planted
The blossom grows
Out of the darkness
Beauty flows
Year after year
More fragrant is this rose
Many come and marvel
A one-of-a-kind flower
A strong stem
Gained in seasons' showers
With roots in firm foundation
It stands strong
Its leaves dancing to the melody of the breeze
Then it's time for the Sower to reap and harvest what He's grown
Leaving the scented fragrance of its existence to the beloved left alone.
Uncle Wendell was that flower uprooted
My tears flow at such a loss
Why oh why did God not let us keep what He'd sown?
Be Still He says
He is with me now to rest

Dry your tears
And praise the years
He was a mighty husband, father, cousin and son
He was an awesome uncle and friend to the end
My heart is broken but I force a smile
As I think of all the memories of him from whence I was
a child.

My loving and humorous Uncle Wendell

Mummy, I Am Here

Your beauty of how you love me
Has not gone amiss
I come to you daily with a heavenly kiss
Thanking you, Mummy, for being the one
Thanking God for choosing me to be your son

We laughed, we played
And I know you prayed
Giving glory to God for all He has done
I see you cry day after day
I know it's hard, but Mummy, it's going to be ok

You may not hear people's comforting words
It's hard for them to know what to say
Have patience with them, Mummy, for they love you so
And the pain of losing me they'll never know

Rise up, you really are strong
To shine a smile in the day really isn't wrong
Your strength and your tenacity God has given to you

Just open your eyes and see He is leading you

I do miss your hugs and your scrumptious dinners

Our fun our times together
Every dish to me was a winner
Try not to cry, Mummy
Feel me near
My love surrounds you in the atmosphere

I dance, I jump, I even have piggyback rides
I softly play with you as I live in your mind
Think of this, Mummy
Jesus lives in you, but I live with Him
You see how easy it is to feel me within?

Today's a new day
Lay the weakness of grief aside
The severity of your loss cannot be denied
Our love for each other only to God we can confide.

I'll always be with you in good times and bad
Remember our laughter and try not to be sad
Gather up your garments
Refresh your face
Stand tall, for you, Mother, are a woman of faith

Keep pressing on, oh mother of mine
And as the day falls into another
You'll be just fine.

Twenty-One Days With God

Enlighten me, Lord
Show me, guide me
Let Your light be what I see
My purpose given on my bended knees

I come to You with an open heart
My desire to get this right from the very start
Let my fast be a testimony
May others be filled
Lord, set us free

As I pray and build an alter, I humbly lay
Listening tentatively to what You have to say
God Almighty, have Your way
Be with me as I walk this walk for 21 days

Realign my posture
And let me continue to venture after You, come what may
In Your hands I place my life
I honour You,

Help me to sacrifice all that is superfluous and elaborate to
my taste and sight
Help me through these days

And give me sound sleep at night.
In Your Matchless Glory, mercies for evermore
Watch over me just like when **Abraham offered Isaac**
on the threshing floor
I offer myself as I knock on Your door
Laying aside all my desires and habits, may they keep me
bound no more.
Amen

Gold

Wow
If I knew then what I know now
Would I have a greater smile?
As I sit before the camera
And ponder for a while,
How should I pose?
Should I sit or should I stand
Cross my legs, place my hands
And hide away the pain?
For to expose it brings shame.

Married so long, but something went wrong
The melody of two does not sing the same song
Dressed in gold
I sat majestically
Letting thoughts unfold...
And I released a smile
To have and to hold
In sickness and health
In poverty and in wealth
For better, but my goodness
When it became worse
We came off course

Calling out to God
He clothed me in gold
Wrapped His arms around me
And said, daughter be restored
He also took His son and mended his heart
Changed the direction of his walk
Stripped him of the Spirit of strife
And in God's love, he changed his life.

If I knew then what I know now
I would have lifted my hands to Jesus from the very start
Whisper to Him gently to please collect my tears
Heal our broken hearts
Let us recognise our wrongs
Teach us to humbly say I'm sorry
And in unity sing a brand-new song.
I would trust in my Saviour
My husband would have searched for Him in prayer
In the midst of the darkness

I know He would have met us there
To be robed in diamonds, emeralds or pearls,
Shining silver or the highest karat of gold
None can compare to the Jewel in the Crown
God's Son, Jesus, who allowed us to overcome.

If I knew then what I know now
The meaning of my smile would not be of an inner pain
But one of which says, 'It's ok, God is on our side'

The advisory prowled around
Searching for a crack to reach in
he came and launched an attack
And we forgot we were each other's next of kin
Marriage vows destroyed and in the devil's bin.
But God came into my life
He showed me things and made me understand
It was the enemy that played us

But guess what? he didn't win
Although no longer married
We remain good friends
He prays for me, and I pray for him
One day he will give his life to Christ
And enter in.

If I knew then what I know now
I would put on a dress coloured gold
And smile with a sparkle
Knowing that Christ lives within
Dispelling darkness
Letting go of the madness

And trusting solely in Him

If I only knew.

Farewell My Friend

I hear you in the midst of your favourite songs
My mind goes into a dance
Memories have me in a trance
Do I want to break my imagination
There's a hesitation
I stop

A tear fills my eye as I remember the last goodbye
As we stood in prayer
And I spoke gently in your ear
You responded
With a slight groan
You let us know our presence was known

We've been catapulted,
Watching you get weaker had us devastated
Now we stand and celebrate our dearly beloved
Your life
Your goals
Your smile

Your dreams

I've learnt in life
Nothing is always as it seems
One day laughing, dancing
Entertaining
And the next receive clinical news
That takes out life's light
Like a worn-out fuse

Today we bid you farewell
Friends old and new
Family, all were there to celebrate you
A life well lived
And I count it a privilege
To have known and befriended
Someone as marvellous as you.

Now rest eternally
In the mansion with your name on it
But as you gather with the angels in praise
Look around, have a good gaze

Watch for him especially...
You know who... Andy
Kiss and hug him for me
Then dance together
For you are now both free

Rest In Peace My Friend

My Graduation

Ok...so I'm still on honeymoon (That's what it feels like)

Here I am
Who am I, you ask...

I am a woman who kept her word
To the brother whose voice she heard
No matter what troubles and trials came
I had to finish this for his name.

I am a woman who strives to reach the top
Along the way the enemy fired shots
Yes, I stumbled but I never once totally dropped

I am a woman who cried with uncontrollable grief
When my brother's life unexplainably ceased
The memory of that Good Friday will never go away
But my brother's love within us shall forever stay

I am a woman who believes in vows
Somehow one broke and to that relationship I took a bow
For nothing was going to hold me back and steal my God
given strength
That, my Heavenly Father would not allow

I am a woman who wanted to show her children
That no matter what circumstances they get in,
With God, whatever they put their hands to,
They will accomplish and in years to come be graduating.

I am a woman who fought her own brain
To the point I felt I was doing this all in vain
But my brother's voice I heard again and again
And God held me up so I could shake off the chain of
stroke from hemiplegic migraines

He healed me physically, mentally, emotionally and spiritually

He was the Keyboard, the Laptop, my Tutor, my Father,
my Friend
My Doctor, my Lawyer whose case He did defend
Justice was in sight
And with God I saw this through right...
Yes, right to the end.

Who am I?
I am a woman just like you!
I'm an overcomer, What God did for me He can surely do
for you
I'm a survivor,
What is sent to stop you, kill you, will not get through,
For God's armour has been set in the right position to
protect you.
I'm a winner, a victor, a mother, a friend

I'm a sister, an auntie
My titles have no end
So, I say to you today...

Who are you?
A lawyer
A banker
A surgeon
A leader
A counsellor
A developer... You see, the potential in you is there, this just names a few
I can see it, God can see it
Open your eyes and believe it too
With God you can be allllll what He made you to be
Step out in Faith
I DID
The road was not easy
At times I felt queasy
The enemy hit hard but don't let that put you off
GO FOR IT...
Aspire to aim Higher and God will bring out your wings
Who am I?
I am Alison Maria Ryan-Chase
A Bachelor of Science Environmental Health Graduate 2017
This by far is the BEST year I have ever seen.
Be encouraged

Blessed are those who mourn, for they shall be comforted

—Matthew 5:4

But I would strengthen you with my mouth,
And the comfort of my lips would relieve your grief.

—Job 16:5

But thanks be to God, who gives us the victory through our Lord Jesus Christ.

—1 Corinthians 15:57

Oh, sing to the Lord a new song!
For He has done marvellous things;
His right hand and His holy arm have gained
Him the victory.

—Psalms 98:1

Love suffers long and is kind; love does not envy; love does not parade itself, is not puffed up; 5 does not behave rudely, does not seek its own, is not provoked, thinks no evil; 6 does not rejoice in iniquity, but rejoices in the truth; 7 bears all things, believes all things, hopes all things, endures all things.

—1 Corinthians 13:4-7

10
AS WE CLOSE

Out Flew the Butterfly

Slowly slowly on her belly she moves forward
Refusing to wear the title of coward
She'll try and try
Yes, she will get by
In tiredness may stop and may sigh
She might even look up and think
How can I reach up? The sky is so high
But God said He never made her to crawl
He saw her willingness and created a ball

Inside He placed her delicately
There she waited patiently
And as time stayed still
Waiting on God's will
Change was taking place
Within her heart mind and soul was Spirit filled
Braking away the old
He reformed her like clay
The ball became too small
Encased she needed to break free
So used the new tools He gave her to flee

Beauty beheld her eyes as she stretched
There were two artistic helpers attached

Dreams of reaching the sky
Old body gone,
It was now a reality
The Caterpillar could now fly high!
Go where she wants to go
Yes, be what she wants to be
Began as a caterpillar
But that's not what God had planned for her destiny

Transformation had to take place
Humility learnt with fullness of grace
On her belly was not her place
She was to aim higher and seek His face
Out flew the butterfly
No limits
No hesitation
She has a new and favourable destination.

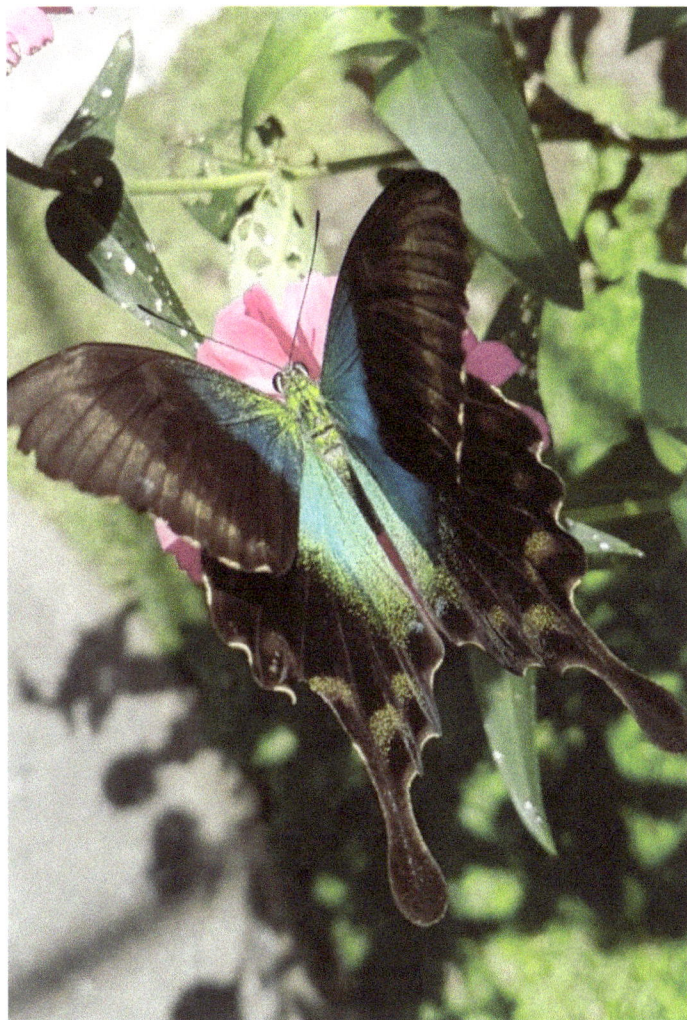

Downloads From Heaven

Doing something, anything
And just like that, it comes
Sweeping down like snowdrops falling from the clouds
I grab a pencil or a pen
And any paper that's in sight
Now equipped, I start to write

Snow drops of letters form the words
I put into sentences all that I have heard
A silent voice whispers in the wind
Telling me all that I write is what is held deep within
Prayers of intercession opened the gates of heaven
Poetic love letters to touch my brethren

I write, sometimes type
To be honest, I just go with the flow
My hands and fingers aren't mines
This I know
The spirit awakes and speaks to set me free
Writing away all bondage
Loosening me from captivity

Emotions of grief
From abuse and loss
That crippled my heart because
Letting go was hard to do
I didn't know then
I could not comprehend

As I gave my life and prayed that summer's day
You, Jesus, shone a light and showed me the way
You spoke words into my soul
Downloads from heaven to make me whole
Using molten gold to seal the cracks
And filled me with the Holy Spirit
You saw beauty in my soils and did that
How could anyone tell me there is no God
When I reveal my many testimonies
Not just I,
But many souls here in this world
And those left to go to the sweet by and by
The story of the cross is very real
Jesus paid a great cost for us who were lost
Internally, we now can heal

The first to demonstrate the art of Kintsugi
Every broken piece of my clay
Pieces of debt, loss, broken relationships
Pieces of betrayal, ill health and diminished wealth
Pieces of broken dreams…

God, with His infinite love
Took the pieces and gave them new names
One called Joy the other Peace, Kindness, Goodness
Some called Faithful and Good,
Longsuffering but with an added name of Self-Control
A name of Gentle but the greater was called Love
Which God, in my deliverance
Sealed with His Son's blood

Fruits of the Spirit in one breath is my name
Now I walk with no shame
My past is in the sea of forgetfulness
Now I stand and proclaim
Jesus is the answer for you too
No matter your culture
Create an alter
He will send downloads from heaven
And I promise you, you will never be the same
The Holy Spirit will come and live in you
His voice shall lead the way.

.

Acknowledgments

How can I finish this collection without giving praise to my Lord And Saviour Jesus Christ? I have much gratitude that He allowed the Holy Spirit to intercede on my behalf, downloading a symphony of words to make music through these pages like a symbolic orchestra. God put scriptures in my heart that resonated with the subjects of the poems I have written.

So, to the Trinity, I give my first words of gratitude.

I give thanks to my five beautiful children who never stop believing in me and aspiring me to aim higher—my number one cheerleaders! I love you all dearly.

My closest friends have also been instrumental in encouraging me to write, too many, but Bernadette, thank you for all your words that made me feel capable. You've been there since we were sixteen and I hold dear to my heart, 'The Finger-Cheek Pose'.

My extended family, mum, my siblings, my nieces, nephews and cousins. Thank you for your constant support and love. I love how we are a tight bunch.

To my pastors who have spoken words over my life concerning writing books. Thank you for being that vessel that God used to push me into my calling. I realise my purpose and how I shall touch and encourage many souls to seek the Lord and gain healing after reading my words.

Finally, I wish to thank my publisher, Daniella Blechner, and her team at Conscious Dreams Publishing. Their expertise, love for people, talents and relentless help towards me reaching my goal deserve much commendation. I could not have produced this book without you all.

About the Author

Alison Ryan-Chase is a mother of five, lovingly known as 'Granny Ali' to four and mother-in-law to two. Married and divorced twice, Alison has lived a life filled with trials and triumphs.

After suffering a stroke in 1999 and losing her speech, cognitive and motor skills, Alison taught herself to talk and walk again as well as to do one of the things she feels most passionate about. Cooking.

One of her biggest achievements is that despite battling ill health, marital strife and dealing with overwhelming grief from the loss of her dearly beloved brother in 2012, she managed to obtain a Bachelor of Science degree in Environmental Health.

Alison is a professional chef with over 35 years of experience and is now the proud personal chef of a fine dining business called Palys G2:9.

Alison has a passion for writing and has poured out her innermost thoughts with guidance from above. 'Downloads from Heaven' is her first book of many more to come.

Conscious Dreams

PUBLISHING

Transforming diverse writers
into successful published authors

www.consciousdreamspublishing.com

authors@consciousdreamspublishing.com

Let's connect